Visit us on the web at datingafterdivorcebook.com

NEVER AGAIN!

DATING AFTER DIVORCE:
HOW TO PROTECT YOURSELF, YOUR CHILDREN AND YOUR ASSETS

JAMES M. GRAHAM AND CATHERINE ONEIL

Never Again!

Dating After Divorce: How to Protect Yourself, Your Children and Your Assets

By James M. Graham and Catherine Oneil

Table of Contents

Disclaimer 7

Who is this book for? 8

Why we chose this subject to write about? 9

What will this book do for you? 10

Chapter 1: Are You Ready To Date? 12

Chapter 2: How To Screen Your Dates 22

Chapter 3: Protect Yourself Online 30

Chapter 4: Relationship is Mantra 41

Chapter 5: Attraction 56

Chapter 6: Preserve Your Assets the Second Time Around 68

Chapter 7: The Financially Irresponsible Future Spouse 84

Chapter 8: Unmarried Couples And Their Finances
                     Let's get it right! 89

Chapter 9: Prenuptial Agreements 105

Chapter 10: How To Make Sure Your Loved Ones
                       Are Protected 115

Chapter 11: Legacy Planning 122

Chapter 12: Keeping Assets In Your Family If Your
                       Child Is Financially Irresponsible 135

Chapter 13: Protect Your Children's College Money 139

Chapter 14: Long Term Care Protection 142

Chapter 15: Mistakes Investors Make 152

Course 165

About The Authors 167

Industry Disclosures 169

Disclaimer

This book is for informational purposes only and does not give tax or legal advice. Laws vary per state. Federal and state laws are subject to change. It is important to seek professional advice for your specific situation. The purpose of this book is to educate. The authors shall not have any liability or responsibility to any person or entity with respect to any loss or damage caused, or alleged to be caused, directly or indirectly, by the information contained in this book.

Who is this book for?

This book is for those who have come out of a long-term relationship or marriage (divorce, separation or death) and want to get back into the dating world. Whether you are seeking a long-term relationship or a casual one, you will find this book helpful for the emotional and practical advice, tips and examples that will guide you toward the relationships and love you desire, while protecting yourself, your children and your assets.

Those of you who have not had traumatic experiences in past relationships will find this information very useful to help avoid the difficulties others have experienced.

This book will help you move past your fear of relationships. In addition, it can prevent you from repeating mistakes. Next, it will guide you toward attracting the love and security you desire.

Why we chose this subject to write about?

In our respective fields, as a relationship counselor and a financial planner, we have seen many people who have gone through extremely difficult divorces and break-ups. Often such circumstances leave people emotionally, physically and financially devastated. It's not just the two of us who see these "walking wounded." We all know someone who has gone through this—people who have suffered things like psychological or physical abuse. Maybe you're aware of children who are used by one parent against another, or theft of a family member's money. The emotional and financial pain can linger far longer than the time it takes to get out of a bad situation. The long-term effects can be devastating to children who may absorb the pain and abuse drugs as a coping mechanism, or develop other addictive and destructive habits. They may become just like their abusive parent, or embody a "victim mentality" for life. It can become an endless cycle from one generation to the next.

This is our attempt to break that cycle and help people become more aware of problems before they occur.

Our combination of these two seemingly separate concepts— emotional and financial—may seem unusual, but they often go hand-in-hand, especially when it comes to relationships.

What will this book do for you?

This book will help you:

1. Gain clarity of the dating process after coming out of a divorce or a break-up.
2. Identify who is seriously looking for a relationship so you do not waste your time.
3. Understand your prior relationship patterns, so you can avoid making the same mistakes.
4. Protect yourself from online predators.
5. Learn how to tell if your date is emotionally healthy.
6. Identify your relationship blind spots.
7. Protect your sexual health.
8. Protect your children in the dating process.
9. Be more aware during the dating process.
10. Overcome dating-related anxiety.
11. Know when you're revealing too much, too soon.
12. Attract a loving healthy relationship by knowing what questions to ask.
13. Be more perceptive during the dating process.
14. Ensure that your needs are met in a relationship.
15. Know why you have been attracting the partners you have been attracting.
16. Protect your assets in future relationships.
17. Learn how to leave money to your children/ grandchildren without that money being wasted.

18. Learn how to financially provide for yourself and your children when getting into a new relationship.

19. Merge money when getting into a long-term relationship or marriage.

20. Know when it's okay to let your significant-other assist you with aspects of your finances.

21. Avoid mistakes investors commonly make.

22. Determine if you should have a prenuptial agreement.

23. Help you decide if you should sign a prenuptial agreement.

24. Get comfortable discussing prenuptial agreements.

25. Protect yourself from a financially irresponsible partner.

26. Protect your assets, reduce taxes, and provide for the members of a blended family.

27. Reduce the risk of long-term care expenses that can deplete your assets and place a heavy burden on your family.

28. Protect your children's college money.

29. Protect your adult children's money from themselves.

30. Reduce your liability from your children's mistakes.

31. Reduce the chances your child will need expensive rehab.

Chapter 1

Are You Ready To Date?

Q **What are the dangers of dating too soon after the relationship ends?**

A **In today's world, many people are dating after years of being married.** Unfortunately, they are often dating before they have learned their own role in their last, failed relationship. We call this "ego dating." It's like picking your next mate while wearing earplugs and a blindfold.

Here's a real-life example from my practice. (Names have been changed for confidentiality). John filed for divorce after discovering his wife was having an affair. Unfortunately, John never received any help to recover from this stressful event. In addition, he lost half his assets in the divorce, but his real pain is in missing his children. He lives in a no-fault divorce state and has one night a week and every other weekend visits with his children. This is a sad situation, but the problem is John never learned what role he played in contributing to his dysfunctional marriage. He believes everything that went wrong with his marriage is his wife's fault. This kind of victim thinking is likely to only attract another victimizing situation. John now looks at all women as cheaters until proven otherwise.

The subconscious mind wants to avoid pain at all costs, and has a funny way of protecting against perceived threats. This makes John susceptible to victimizing his future dates. This type of person might use women sexually, or become impotent (on a subconscious level) as a way to punish women.

In his current state, John would not be a good catch. To effectively move forward, he would need to accept responsibility for his part of the failed marriage. What might that be? After working with John, I was able to discover that he jumps into relationships entirely too soon. He tends to make decisions strictly on the physical level without assessing a person's emotions or value system. John made many assumptions about his wife without verifying, or by basing his decisions on the wrong criteria. For example, he decided she was a good choice for him because of her high-paying salary and status in the community.

Until a person reflects on his or her own role in the causes of a divorce, that person is not a healthy date.

As you're getting back into the dating game, it is important to know that you should avoid any date who solely blames his or her spouse for a failed marriage, without taking any responsibility. You will only be a target for this person's unresolved anger.

Takeaway: Avoid the angry man or woman!

Q **What should I consider when dating after a divorce?**

A **Many people rush into finding a lifetime partner too soon after a divorce.** Men especially are more inclined to jump right back into the fire. They often have a checklist when picking a partner. The problem is that checklist is never long enough. Any partner you pick will bring both pain and pleasure into your relationship. Unfortunately, too many people live in a fantasy world thinking that anyone will be better than their ex-spouse.

1. Do not pick your next partner before you have learned your role in your previous failed relationship. Doing so will only increase the chances of another disastrous relationship. If you are still blaming your ex-spouse for your unhappiness then you are not conscious enough to pick your next partner.

    A man who is still wounded is extremely vulnerable and can fall victim to the exact same experience they just got out of. A wounded male should treat his wounds before re-entering the dating world. If not he will be picking a woman on an analytical level rather than from his heart. Every behavior his partner exhibits will be compared to his previous partner and filtered through his wounded judgment—thus resulting in yet another unconscious choice. If a man's decision is fear-based when choosing a woman it means he does not trust his own judgment.

2. Seek a partner who is in control of his or her emotions. Julie meets a man named Eric at a business party. He is attractive, articulate, educated and fun to be with. They go out several more times and every time they go out alcohol is present. Julie has yet to have a date where alcohol is not in the picture. She has a false sense of reality about Eric's personality. She assumes he holds down a full-time job. He seems happy and looks good.

    Later on while driving to the beach, Eric screams at Julie for forgetting to pack something. She is in shock at the way he is treating her. She then realizes that Eric is only happy when he has a few drinks in him. Happiness is a choice in life. Unfortunately, too many people hide behind false vices that are discovered later. These can be hidden by mental health prescriptions, alcohol, drugs or a strong physical attraction.

3. A man can be blinded by a pretty physique and miss the fact that a woman is missing a soul. Unfortunately, he does not realize that until later when he catches her screwing her personal trainer in their bed. Many partners just assume that their mate has morals because they project their morals on the other person. Some may find out for the first time

they are unloved when they lose their financial assets or get a devastating cancer diagnosis. They might go decades before finding out their partner never loved them.

4. Seek a partner with a positive mental attitude regardless of what obstacles God throws his or her way. Life comes with challenges and a partner who has the ability to overcome adversity and display resilience goes a long way.

5. A person who lacks any sort of passion will expect his partner to make him happy. A relationship with this expectation will be doomed once he grows bored. A man with this expectation is living in a fantasy world expecting the woman to be responsible for his happiness. He can easily fall prey to substance abuse or process addictions when his relationship stops fulfilling his needs. He might seek outside happiness in porn, sex, video games, work or gambling.

6. The last thing a person needs is to jump right back into another unhealthy relationship. The more conscious you can be in the dating process, the less chance of encountering another disastrous relationship!

Q How do I avoid the "rebound relationship"?

A **Many people have trouble being alone after a relationship ends.** Often they jump right back into the fire convinced that this time they have figured things out.

Max was married to a beautiful woman who was sleeping with everyone but Max. He had paid for all of her plastic surgeries and unfortunately didn't notice who all of it was for. Max found out the hard way by walking in on her and his accountant. He found it odd since the accountant was not her type. He later learned she wanted the books fudged to inflate a future business valuation in an upcoming planned divorce. There were plenty of warning signals, but he had chosen to ignore them.

After experiencing a traumatic painful event like this, the subconscious mind goes into protection mode. It wants to assure that Max never again faces this much emotional pain.

Max then starts dating Molly who looks and acts very conservative. Her bland style of dress with the absence of plastic surgery results in a false sense of security.

Many people make the mistake of picking an extreme opposite mate after a painful relationship. They rationalize that they just picked the wrong type of mate and will screen better next time. And they end up with someone even further away from what they want.

Now, Max is safe but his decision to enter a relationship based on fear rather than love results in even more misery. His mind has linked an attractive female to pain in his perception. He now feels much safer with women who are less attractive.

The brain can play many games on us when we experience painful events. There are many triggers from painful experiences, and the mind retains most of them. If you are dating, know that you too have many points of reference when it comes to choosing a significant other. One reason a decent relationship is hard to find is because so many have no idea what one even looks like.

When entering your next relationship thoroughly consider if a date is too much of an extreme from what you initially had chosen. Often, you are reacting to the prior painful event and you really might actually want to be somewhere in the middle. Max learned the hard way since he is now feeling safe but lives with a dull, boring woman. His mind linked dull and boring to less emotional pain. Pain can be displayed in multiple ways in relationships. The next time you enter a relationship, evaluate whether the relationship initiated from a fear-based decision or a love-based decision. Decisions based on fear will often get you into trouble.

Q **What is the most important relationship in your life?**

A **It is not uncommon to hear people complain about their significant other.** When people are in pain they tend to blame others for how they are feeling. This can go on for quite some time and can keep someone running in circles. Anger is often the predominant emotion when one feels unloved. Unresolved anger will always keep one stuck in the past. It also keeps a person from seeing any possible solutions.

Anger will run one's life decisions while reason and logic get left behind.

What most do not realize is that the anger is usually self-directed. We are really angry at ourselves for staying in an unhealthy relationship. If only we had learned decades earlier that we were really angry at ourselves.

Most have no idea what a healthy relationship looks like.

Our reference point on love is modeled from our family of origin. Intimate communication skills are also modeled from the previous generation.

People can spend decades blaming others for their struggles and unhappiness. The defense mechanism of blame keeps them from finding true joy in their lives.

The absolute most important relationship you have is the one you have with yourself. If your self-esteem has been damaged, you will select a mate that matches your belief system.

Life is a lesson on gaining self-esteem and self-love. A person will continue to attract unhealthy mates until one gains the self-love and self-esteem to see the truth and walk away.

 What are the mistakes women make when dating?

 Across America, women are re-entering the dating pool after years of being married. Unfortunately, this can produce extreme anxiety for some. A common mistake of many is to think that all you have to do is bring looks and a halfway decent body to your future partner. The world is way more competitive these days and much more is required than looks and a nice physique.

Thanks to online dating, men are like little kids in a candy store with all their options. Some women text nude photos to potential suitors. Some foreign women are willing to do anything for a green card. There are numerous websites and apps for a quick free sexual encounter.

Men today have numerous women to choose from and women need to be a bit more evolved. It is important to examine exactly what you have to offer a man beyond just looks and a body. Ask yourself: Are you in a stable career? Do you have your own dreams and goals? Or are you looking for Mr. Right to rescue you from your mounting debt and be responsible for your happiness?

Make a list of everything you have to offer your future mate. Are your emotions in balance? Are you okay being alone, or are you jumping into a relationship due to boredom and fear of the unknown? This scenario makes women settle, and is a set-up for future misery.

The more empowered a woman is in the seven areas of life (social, vocational, financial, physical, mental, spiritual, and career), the lower the odds that she will feel less power in a new relationship. As a woman, if you want to raise the caliber of men you attract then examine where you are weak and get empowered in that area. Women who are financially dependent are at risk of being overpowered in their relationships.

Have you ever heard the saying, "Those who make the gold make the rules?"

Get empowered!
Don't settle for anything less than love!

Chapter 2

How To Screen Your Dates

 What are the dating mistakes commonly made after being married?

 Answer for women:

Have you ever noticed how a mate could win an Academy Award during the dating process? An inner voice is saying this guy is just too good to be true. He opens doors, listens, shows respect, talks to you and acts like a gentleman. Next, he genuinely acts like he actually cares about your children. He is charismatic, nice-looking and wins over your friends and family.

Even though everything appears to be going well you are ignoring vital warning signs—possible signals such as the feeling an emotional vampire just sucked your entire energy field.
You might feel scattered and unproductive in your personal life.
You might wake up even more tired than when you went to bed.

Unfortunately many people fail to realize how much another human being can drain one's energy field. If it is a healthy union, one should be energized and inspired by his or her partner. The problem arises when a manipulative partner is not recognized due to his or her Academy Award-winning performance. One needs to watch out for the 5 signs below!

1. He announced too soon that this is a committed relationship. Even though your heart desires a relationship, run for the hills if this is forced upon you. This is a sign he is profoundly insecure.

2. Even though you have only been dating for a few months he is already talking about being with you 25 years from now.

3. He tries to take every second of your time, leaving no time or energy for friends or family. Next, he gives you guilt trips if you decline, or demands your schedule with an itemized itinerary.

4. He tries to buy you an iPhone so that he can install the Follow Me app and know exactly where you are at all times. It is a federal offense in some states for parties to use phones for tracking that do not belong to them. Some people will install Flexi-spy so they can read your emails and texts.

5. He tries to get you to share personal details about your life way too soon in case you're planning on escaping the relationship.
    If any of these traits sound familiar, then recognize you are lacking important boundaries in your life. Never drop what

is important to you such as your life's dreams and goals. Do not make yourself too available for anyone. Many people so want to be loved that they will jump through hoops just to get attention. Unfortunately, being too nice can lead to very undesirable situations.

If he looks too good to be true then time to assess your energy level around him!

 Answer for men:

It is not unusual for a person to have a mental checklist of desired traits for a significant other. The most common traits--physical beauty, intelligence, personality, education and career status--are all highly rated. Some might go for strong physical attraction and ignore the rest of the list.

Unfortunately, many never even create a checklist. They accept the first person who shows up at the door.

The divorce rate is close to 67% for second marriages. Men are usually first to be remarried after a divorce. Often their choices are based on women's physical attributes when they have yet to take adequate time to heal from a prior divorce. Many have not yet dropped the anger from their prior spouses to properly evaluate a future significant other. This in turn leaves men extremely vulnerable to becoming victimized once again in another unhappy and unsatisfying relationship.

Many men can become blinded by a strong physical attraction and end up with a woman they thought they knew. (This is even more common with men coming out of a cold sexless marriage.) Traits that are often missed are selfishness, mental illness, self-centeredness, controlling, manipulative, drama queen, and emotional instability.

Men who are the rescuing type can end up with a total train wreck. Their strong desire to be needed can land them with an emotionally immature women that drains every ounce of his energy.

Picking a wounded mate is the same as picking a person who is not living in present-day reality. Her unbalanced emotional state will eventually rub off on his career and health as well. The wounded mate should be avoided-- the majority will be resentful of having to be rescued in the first place. Her internalized anger over needing to be rescued will likely result in a severe lack of gratefulness for his kind actions.

Universal law will predict what type of woman a man draws into his life. If he is too loving and caring, he will attract a cold fish to bring him in balance. When we are out of balance, the universe will bring us the perfect mate, when we learn to love ourselves more. When we truly love ourselves, we do not always have to be the one giving in the relationship.

Avoid the wounded mate! You deserve better!

Who attracts an abusive mate?

Unfortunately, an abusive mate does not come with warning signs like, "Danger Ahead." They can be male or female, and come from all levels of socioeconomic status. The damage they cause can span multiple generations because their children often model either the victim or the abuser's behavior.

There are multiple factors involved in picking an abusive mate. A dysfunctional childhood can be a set up for repeating this. If your emotional and physical needs were unmet as a child then an emotionally unavailable spouse seems normal in your perception. Childhood neglect can also leave a person with an approval addiction. This approval addiction can make an abused spouse stay much longer than someone without the addiction in an abusive relationship.

People with an approval addiction need the support and approval of others. They often have a pleaser personality, which can attract a control freak or superiority complex abuser. They were used to having to beat their head against the wall trying to obtain love as a child. Thus, they are just reacting out this scenario in their adult relationship. Low self-esteem and guilt can also attract an abusive mate.

Infatuation can also blind a person's perception when dating. This highly emotional dopamine state only allows a person to see one side of his or her significant other. Physique, good looks, impressive career or a strong physical attraction can all serve to mask the signs of an abuser. A helpful technique for clarity, when infatuated, is to physically write out 250 drawbacks of a significant other to balance this polarized state.

An emotionally needy person is also prone to abuse. The person might suffer from chronic grief due to the loss of a family member and thus attract an abusive mate. In addition, whenever core beliefs are violated, one can attract into their life an abusive mate due to their subconscious guilt. An abusive person often rushes into an instant relationship. That person will dominate his or her victim's life by alienating him or her from friends and family.

The more a person can love and value him or herself, the less likely he or she will attract an abusive mate. One needs to be in control of their emotions before selecting a significant other.

Q **Who attracts a narcissist?**

A **Every person has a role in the selection of his or her significant other.** A narcissist can't survive without a victim. A victim plays out the "co-dependent mantra"- whereby she never has to be responsible for herself again. There is always a payoff for remaining in this type of a dysfunctional relationship. Victims are easy to spot--they tend to make decisions based on fear. Their predominant thoughts are also fear-based as opposed to love-based. They tend to stay long in dysfunctional relationships.

The fear of the unknown, losing their security, their kids, and their lifestyle keeps them trapped in a web of dysfunction. They also tend to have a great deal of trouble hurting others so they remain suffering in an unhealthy marriage.

The relationship was not always like this. In the beginning, the victim had a strong need for self-approval from others. Self- approval as in, "Tell me 1000 times how much you need me". A person who needs self-approval from others is often slightly unconscious.

One reason a person might need approval from others is because of childhood neglect. One of their parents was emotionally unavailable. This can happen due to addiction or a bad case of detachment from anxiety or depression. It can also happen with an absent parent due to divorce or a workaholic parent. The child develops this pleaser mentality in order to get their needs met. The child assumes that she has done something wrong from the lack of attention from either parent. She now goes over board to get her emotional and physical needs met. In fact, she will put others needs before her own.

A person who attracts a narcissistic mate often attracts narcissistic friends as well. The predominant accommodating personality type is a pleaser. A pleaser has a strong need to be accepted by others. You might find them apologizing even when they have done nothing wrong. Pleasers often assume that everything is their fault even when it is not. "If only I would have done things differently--then maybe my dad would notice that I exist."

The self-absorbed narcissist needs to be able to control and manipulate his victim. The highly critical narcissist will leave the pleaser doubting her ability to do just about anything. The narcissist creates a helpless mate with consistent abusive and critical remarks.

If you are prone to attracting narcissists, break free. In order to do this, a person must recognize that part of him or her which is attracting this abuse. Until we learn to unconditionally love ourselves 100%, we will keep attracting a mate who forces us to love ourselves enough to walk away from the painful abuse.

Mate selection has to do with us and our level of self-esteem. The problem occurs when a victim gets stuck in blaming his or her past mate without taking away the life lesson. No one will love you until you love yourself!

Chapter 3

Protect Yourself Online

Q How do I avoid dating a predator online?

A **Dating in today's world usually starts with a search on Google.** Unfortunately, there are far too many people who are trusting to the point of blindness when meeting a person online. They may drop their guard feeling safe behind a computer screen. Some actually think they are perfectly safe on a reputable dating site that charges money.

An article in the Huffington Post shared a story of a woman who was cleaned out financially by a man she had met online. This woman felt safe since she was on one of the biggest online dating sites in the industry. Her emotional pain from being alone for so long caused her to ignore her inner voice. She had fallen in love too fast and would do anything to make him happy. The dopamine rush of being in love made her oblivious to the situation at hand.

To keep this from happening to you:

1. Avoid any person who rushes too quickly into a relationship. The woman who was ripped off did not see this signals since her ego craved all the attention from this male suitor. She had become trapped in her pain from her previous unhealed relationship which made her easy prey for him to move in for the kill. An abundance of phone calls on a daily basis made her feel as if the man actually cared for her. This is a common strategy for a sociopath to gain control over someone else's emotions.

2. Run if the person discusses marriage too soon. Even though many people desire a soul mate to spend the rest of their life with relationships don't evolve overnight. If the person is already talking about spending the rest of his or her life with you and you have yet to meet in person, run. The woman who got swindled was hearing everything she wanted to hear from the man who ran off with her money. She actually thought her prayers were now answered and she could have the wedding she had always dreamed about.

3. Be extremely cautious of international dates (especially those made online). They can lead to marriages that will get you into serious financial trouble. In case you're not up on the news, there is no lack of potential partners from an economically-depressed country who will be interested in marrying you in order to get into a better financial situation.

This happens to men and women! Then again, many foreigners just want a green card but are acting as if you are the person they always dreamed about. The problem is you do not pick up on that since they are actually asking you to come to their country and live. The ego of their partner fails to recognize this since they love all the attention. This is a ploy since once they marry an American they will get you to move later.

4. Avoid a person who shares too much information too soon. For example, Amy was ecstatic about the new man from Florida that she'd met. He seemed charming, articulate, attractive and easy to talk to. Bill would talk about anything from his investments to his stock portfolio. Amy felt eager to share similar details – including that her house was paid off in full and her retirement was already funded. These are not normal beginning topics of conversation; people with the wrong intentions will open up to see if you will reciprocate information about your assets. In Amy's case, she had no idea that Bill was making everything up and was looking for a woman who could support him. Bill's goal was to marry up; Once married, he could take over and manage the finances.

5. Be careful of any person you haven't yet met who wants to talk for hours on the phone. Be aware of what information you're putting in your online profiles. Words like "widow", posting your birth date, or providing job details can be flags for criminals. Know that criminals can create a variety of fictional profiles to snag vulnerable people.

Trisha was extremely lonely after burying her husband. She was previously married to a cold, boring spouse who would never get off his computer.

Once she entered the online dating world she met Donald. Donald would call several times a day and literally talk for hours. Trisha fell in love over Skype! She was dying of loneliness and Donald was the first man in her life who actually could meet her emotional needs. Her heart would race from just hearing his call on Skype.

Donald chose Trisha because her online profile stated that she was a widow. He was hoping that there would be some left over life insurance to share. The problem is Donald is really in severe debt. He was laid off from his last company for missing too much work. He now calls himself a private consultant so people do not think he is without a job. He needs Trisha since he lacks health insurance and has bad diabetes. Trisha had mentioned that she works for a large hospital and has great benefits such as health and life insurance. He also loved the fact that she was a nurse and could take care of him one day.

Unfortunately, Trisha was a bit clueless for disclosing too much information on her profile. A widow can be an open target for a predator. She has no clue why Donald is really smothering her with so much attention.

Love does not happen overnight, but a dependent relationship does! Predators can be male or female. If you want to avoid meeting a predator online, list your occupation as law enforcement. You can always explain later that you wanted to protect your children as well as yourself. A predator is more likely to run from a person who can do a fast and comprehensive background check on him or her.

Q **How do I screen my online dates?**

A **There are now over 54 million single people dating online in America.** Many are coming out of failed marriages looking for another try at love. In 2013, 17% of all marriages occurred from online dating sites.

One thing to screen for is a person with an addictive personality. What, if any, are their addictions? An addiction is an unconscious habit and can be from any source. There are addictions from substances like alcohol or drugs. There are process addictions which do not involve substances, but activities that take over one's life and prevent someone from being emotionally available. Process addictions include eating disorders, gambling, work, porn, Internet, video games, sex, even shopping.

An addictive personality type has difficulty dealing with stress. Assess in advance how your date reacts to stress? Does he or she fly off the handle and lose their cool? Or do they blame you, telling you that everything is your fault? Why not purposely miss a flight or an exit on the freeway while late to a movie and assess the response?

A person who cannot deal with minor stress will have you walking on egg shells. How does he or she deal with difficult or tense situations? Are you scolded like a child? Does the person drink like a fish? Many people are purposely on their best behavior, so challenging them can let you know what the future might hold.

People with mental illness often display quick changes in their mood. It is the inability to handle one's emotions which lead to the mental breakdown. Next, assess for any social withdrawal or a change in sleeping or eating habits. Do they display any prolonged sadness? Depression is often seen in people who lack goals in life. Excessive worrying can be seen with an anxiety disorder. Delusions or paranoia can be a major red flag as well. Can she hold a job, or does she change jobs frequently?

Next, assess any changes in work, family, or relationships. Has the person blown off his or her children entirely to spend all his or her time with you? Perhaps the children might just shed light on your future Mr. Prince Charming. Do not let your ego be filled with all his gracious attention. Does he take you to visit his family or avoid them like the plague? Consider going on a vacation and assess his behavior and what medications he brings? Better to find out now than to be surprised at a later time.

A co-dependent person is also a set-up for mental illness and addiction. He or she may make you responsible for his or her happiness. It is imperative that you not be the only source of happiness for your mate. Your mate needs to have his or her own dreams and goals or else you will be paying the price to keep your partner entertained.

John was a bit apprehensive to date after divorcing a woman with a shopping addiction. He is still paying off half of her credit card debt. His over-focus on fear will most likely land him another emotionally unavailable woman.

John actually needs to drop his fear of attracting yet another mentally unstable mate. The more he can focus on the qualities he desires in a woman, the better his dates will be. A person attracts a mate who is as emotionally available as he or she is. Meditation, yoga, and getting in touch with one's inner voice (intuition) will increase the odds of attracting a healthier mate.

Focus on the qualities you want to attract!

 What are the drawbacks of online dating?

Many of you have seen the commercials which state that one-fourth of all marriages today occur as a result of online dating. However, many of the other seventy-five percent remain frustrated with the online dating fiasco.

One drawback of the online dating process is that many people on dating sites are still zombies recovering from their last torturous relationship. This group tends to search for a mate as if they are in a mine-field waiting for something to explode. Any possible comment that sniffs of the old spouse can result in them canceling all contact with you. Others may offer no information—they barely write anything so no one can ever get close to them again.

Some can also suffer from anxiety and panic attacks from the fear of dating and attracting yet another abusive spouse or possible gold digger. She might talk excessively as a form of self-sabotage since her last relationship was so traumatizing. Excessive talking is actually a common problem that is easily fixed with hypnosis. The brain remembers how much pain was inflicted from the last relationship so the fear of getting involved again has to be cleaned out of the subconscious mind.

You also might hear a pretty good voice fluctuation of anger or contempt for the mere questioning about their ex-lover. Then there are the ones who do not want to be asked any questions since they have just been put through extensive litigation and depositions. They are in fear of your motives behind the personal questions about their employment.

What can a person do to prevent their last torturous relationship from interfering with one's love life?

Many who live in fear tend to respond by intellectualizing rather than coming from one's heart. It can help a great deal to not respond right away until you have time to reread that email. You can also put your hand on your heart and see if you would write the same response as you did when you just fired off that email without thinking of the consequences.

One thing that can be very helpful when going through the online dating process is to not come from judgment. A woman who has been put down by her husband might perceive any comments on her work as a possible threat. A man might perceive any questions about his occupation as a gold digger's interrogation after having written a big check to his ex-wife. If any of these scenarios sound familiar to you, then chances are you still have some healing to do!

When dating, it would be helpful to avoid questions about the ex-spouse. Instead, ask what the person likes to do for fun? Avoid chasing away a person you like because you are on a flaw-finding mission to eliminate any perceived ex-spouse characteristics.

When it comes to love one needs to make decisions from the heart!

Q Men ask:
Why do women ignore my online profile?

A **Have you ever wondered why a woman did not respond to your online dating profile?** Perhaps you thought it was because she gets too much attention from other male suitors? Many men rationalize that pretty women get too many hits, but fail to assess if it is due to the verbiage in their own online profile.

Here are 6 reasons a woman may pass over your profile:

1. John included these must haves in his profile: You must like my football team and listen to my country music! If a man makes these controlling demands he appears selfish and narcissistic. If a person includes words like must or has to, then a woman will usually know who to delete.

2. If your profile includes five traits you cannot live without and sex, satin sheets, intimacy, long weekends in bed, and kissing are your choices, then she will hit Delete. You not only come across as a sex addict but seem 100% on the physical level only. Replace the word sex with love. Women want to be loved but when you only list words like you work at a sex shop store you will be deleted. You just come off as a creepy guy!

3. If your profile goes too in depth with intricate details of how you want to spend your life together you will be deleted. This is not the place to give so much detail and can be

discussed at a later time. Many are too impatient to read a novel on day one and since they do not even know you yet they do not care. This can give the appearance of a man who is too analytical with his laundry list and not in his heart. Plus, it can give off the scent of emotional neediness or loneliness. It is obvious that you wanted a life partner yesterday, but you should appear somewhat of a challenge.

4. If you put your last favorite book read is your last Visa statement, since it had so many pages you will be deleted. She cannot tell if you are bipolar with money management issues or just terrified of encountering a gold digger.

5. Each of your pictures includes alcohol or you doing shots. If you're looking for another potential alcoholic, then chances are you'll meet your soul mate.

6. Do not include pictures with your previous mate blocked or blurred out. It is obvious you are in a hurry since you have no time to take a picture of you alone.

7. Skip any pictures with your shirt off or with you scantily dressed. Women are more cerebral and you appear like a juvenile.

Chapter 4

Relationship is Mantra

Q Why do you deny your inner voice about relationships?

A **A person's inner voice is like a built-in GPS navigational system.** The problem is that many fail to tune into the right frequency. One's inner voice can also be felt by some like that queasy feeling one gets in the pit of their stomach when something doesn't seem right.

The problem is many do in fact recognize these symptoms but actually choose to ignore all of them. This is because our ego cannot deal with the reality that a person we love has no love for us. In the book, "The Magic In Your Mind" by U.S. Anderson, he describes how human behavior can be studied by what a person does to get love.

The subconscious mind has a strong desire to be loved. David adored his wife Lisa and would do anything in the world for her. He excelled in his career so that he could provide a nice life for their family. Lisa rarely showed appreciation for all the nice things David did for her. The more he did for her the more she pulled away.

David sensed something was off but just could not put his finger on it. He decided that it was just a transition many people go through when raising children. Next, he attributed Lisa's lack of physical intimacy to the children as well. He rationalized things would get better as the kid's got a bit older.

David started to have trouble sleeping at night. He then went to an MD to get some sleeping pills. This worked for a while but now he was waking up at four am. His mind was trying to rationalize why Lisa had the energy for aerobics but not for him. His work was also slowing down and his sales were not anywhere near his usual monthly quota's.

David started to get stuck in the mind chatter of his brain. He was wondering why Lisa was always so relaxed when he was feeling impatient and agitated. He dismissed it as a content mother with her small children.

This went on for a few more years. By this time David had been on numerous antidepressants but he just felt numb. Lisa rarely had any one-on-one time with David. He noticed when she kissed him it was as if there was no feeling behind it.

David came home early from work and found Lisa in bed with her personal trainer. He now had his answers why she always had time and energy for aerobics. David was filled with anger and rage at her and himself for living a life without love for so long. He had loved his wife so much that the thought of her not loving him never even crossed his mind.

The conscious mind will rationalize every possible strategy why you are not loved-- like health reasons, family issues, or a spouse's personal issues. You might write off the lack of love to hormonal issues, medication side effects, or a spouse's busy work schedule. The bottom line is your inner voice is never wrong! Your ego is getting in the way of your relationship clarity. David went years living a cold existence. If your spouse is rarely intimate with you then time to wake up and quit making excuses.

Don't live a life without love!

Q **What is the price of infatuation?**

A **Have you ever looked back at your relationships to assess your mistakes?** Tina fell head over heels for Larry. He was charming, educated and appeared genuinely interested in what she had to say. She was flattered by all his attention and wanting to spend time with her. In fact, she was barely able to get her own projects done since they were virtually inseparable. Tina was starved for male attention since her father left home early in her life, due to her parents' divorce.

Even though Larry appeared like a doting partner, she was missing all the warning signs of trouble ahead. Larry was rushing to make it a committed relationship. Next, he would act greatly offended if she wanted to go out with her girlfriends. Tina was missing all these signals since having a man love her was the greatest void in her life.

Tina was confusing dependency and a physical connection with love. She entered a co-dependent relationship with a man who expected her to make him happy. Her strong desire to win back the man who abandoned her years earlier was the perfect set-up for an emotionally needy male.

Tina was living in a fantasy world about relationships. She was only assessing what Larry was doing right in their relationship. She placed him on a pedestal and sublimated his values for hers. Larry liked to go dancing every weekend which Tina hated. She watched football every Sunday because Larry did not like watching it alone.

Tina had forgotten what she likes and values in life and left the path of her own dreams and goals. Tina was planning on finishing her Master's in Nursing. Larry thought if her priorities were in the right place she would abandon that idea and spend every day with him.

Unfortunately, Tina ended up becoming very resentful towards her mate. Her infatuation turned into a nightmare from hell. She had failed to assess the importance of values in a relationship. Larry obviously had a different value system than she did. Tina needed to assess her mate's values before committing to an intimate relationship. In the end, she learned a vital lesson on the importance of personal boundaries and not giving up her goals and dreams.

A new relationship strategy could be, "Flee and they follow versus follow and they flee". She had chosen to follow Larry and now she is fleeing.

If you want the partner of your dreams, then do not give up your own dreams. What you value is just as important as what they value!

Q **What are you learning from your relationship?**

A **Relationships can be like heaven or they can be pure hell.** It has been said that some 95% of intimate relationships are based on fear. Fear-based relationships share common themes: the fear that one is not good enough, smart enough, rich enough, pretty enough or educated enough. This pattern will be seen in the underdog of the relationship. The underdog lives in constant fear that the overdog will leave her if she does not measure up.

Next, the underdog often minimizes herself to the over dog which leaves her extremely vulnerable. She will then subordinate her values for his. This causes a further deterioration in her self-esteem since she is living outside of her values. The more she minimizes herself the more likely her partner will do the same. A lack of respect from her mate is sure to follow. Once she reciprocates a lack of respect for him, the relationship is all but over.

Why is it that so many people feel inferior in their relationships? The reasons can vary from low self-esteem, deep infatuation, or an abusive partner. A mate who only points out faults can incapacitate a sensitive mate. The sensitive mate often gets stuck in her emotions. She fails to assess both sides of the criticism. It is important to look at both sides because criticism can have both positive and negative attributes. The moment one only assesses the negative side is when one gives her power away. "Emotions are lies since they represent incomplete awareness."

Whether you are a man or woman, if you are feeling like the underdog in your relationship, it is time to get out the magnifying glass. Is your spouse's criticism really serving to let you know where to grow? Perhaps this relationship is a life lesson to teach you how to love yourself more. How much pain are you willing to take until you learn that lesson?

Most people live in the fantasy that a relationship is supposed to be happy. The truth is that there will be both pain and pleasure in any relationship. Assess the balance of pain versus pleasure in your relationship. If pain predominates over pleasure, then design a plan of action.

Your choice is to get empowered in that area where you are weak or remain in a painful fear-based relationship. The more empowered one becomes, the less pain one endures. Unfortunately, too many people become trapped in the painful criticism and rarely see it as a growth opportunity to empower their lives.

Don't settle for a fear-based relationship!

 What are your relationship blind spots?

Many single people spend more time researching buying their next car than selecting their next mate.

Our divorce courts are filled with people who are surprised to find out their spouse was not the person they thought they knew. The divorce rate would not be nearly as high as it is if we were more conscious of our mate selection process. Consciousness is when we are fully aware of what we are thinking, saying and doing in our lives.

Many people have a tendency to accept the first mate which walks in the door after being alone. The problem is this may result in settling which can lead to disastrous results.

People tend to make assumptions when selecting a mate. A woman might marry a man she does not completely know. She makes assumptions that he feels the same way about children that she does. Next, she assumes that he honors and respects a committed relationship. Thus, one blind spot is when a trusting person never even considers their spouse a cheater since this is the last thing that would enter her mind. When her husband works long hours she would never doubt his word since her word means something.

Why do we have these blind spots? We all have a perception in our minds of what constitutes a family as well as a significant other. People tend to see only what they wish to see. Blind spots exist to teach us valuable lessons on becoming more conscious in our relationships. Once a person has been scorned by a cheating spouse, one stops assuming everyone is trustworthy.

A man might marry a woman thinking she has restraints when it comes to financial matters. Later, he learns how she knows every sales clerk on a first-name basis at Nordstrom's. He learned the hard way--through her high credit card bills.

Our relationship blind spots often represent our value systems. What we value we assume others value as well. It is because of our false assumptions that we get matched with a person we thought we knew.

If you are about to enter a new relationship, then it is critical to spell out your values and what you want in most areas of your life. If you intend on having children then write out if they think private school is a necessity as well. In addition, assessing how your kids will be disciplined causes many fights as do unruly children. Do not make the assumption that your significant other feels the same as you.

People tend to be money-driven or relationship-driven. Some people value money over relationships and this can destroy a relationship-driven mate. Your discrepancy in values tends to show up later in relationships. For example, a relationship-driven person is attending the funeral of their immediate family member. The money-driven mate does not deem it necessary to take off work since he does not value family and relationships. A relationship-driven person often assumes that their mate feels the same way about family.

A difference in values is what causes many divorces in America! Never assume your mate values what you do! The more you know your own values then you can assess if your mate is on the same page. Unfortunately, most of us learn the hard way by suffering through a painful relationship!

Many people look back on a failed relationship and later realize what they missed. The signs were quite obvious, yet many tend to pretend as if there were none. Why is it that so few of us listen to that inner voice that tells us to run? One reason is because of the timing of our relationships.

One of the absolute worst times to pick a significant other is after a trauma or the loss of a loved one. The death of a loved one leaves a family member extremely vulnerable in many ways. First, their perception is clouded due to the high level of unprocessed negative emotions in the subconscious mind.

Trauma can wipe out a person's self-esteem at the subconscious level. One does not think too highly of themselves after a rape, terminated pregnancy, being fired or burying someone they love. Often times a person can get stuck on the last words that were spoken to the deceased. It plays like a tape in their head over and over reinforcing their guilt.

A grieving family member's sense of perception is so skewed that he can end up with a person he hardly knows. A sense of loss can also leave one searching on just the physical level due to the emotional detachment of the grieving person. An abandonment disorder can also be triggered which produces a great deal of anxiety when left alone. Thus, the person wants to find a quick replacement to fill the painful void.

It is extremely common for a grief stricken person to be filled with subconscious guilt over the death of a loved one. This can result in individuals selecting a mate who will punish them because they think they deserve it. Many people have no idea how much the subconscious mind plays a role in our lives as well as our mate selection. It can have a theme of anger, guilt, shame or fear. It also tends to have either a preponderance of negative or positive emotions. You will not see both.

If your life is not going the way you want it to go then chances are your subconscious mind's negative emotions are running your life. Do you have self-sabotage behavior in relationships? Do you continue to attract the exact same patterns in your mate? If you do, then it might be helpful to clean out any negative emotions with affirmations and/or hypnosis. Next, repeat these positive affirmations 6 to 9 times a day for at least 21 days.

Positive affirmations to enhance your mate selection such as:

- I am attracting a loving relationship that I deserve.

- I love and respect myself.

- I have attracted the perfect partner for me that I deserve.

- I only attract quality people.

Yet, how many times have you heard a person say, "I only attract jerks!," or "I only attract head cases". When people affirm these negative affirmations then they get the same pattern of mates! Analyze what you are affirming about the relationships in your life. We create our own reality from the words that we speak.

Many individuals coming out of a turbulent relationship can have a tendency to overreact when searching for their next mate. The pain serves as a point of reference in one's subconscious mind. Pain or pleasure is how the mind is trained to make sure one does not retreat back to another painful experience.

It is not uncommon after an extremely painful relationship for an individual to seek out possible exit strategies before getting involved with their next mate. The mind is in protective mode and one might be asking in advance,"Will this person be a nightmare to get away from in the event of a future break up?" Some individuals can suffer from mental health disorders that do not fare well when their ego has been deflated. Thus, they seek revenge and retaliation for breaking up with them.

There are warning signals which can show a person in advance who might not be a person to get involved with. One signal is a person who is not comfortable with being alone. Many people look outside of themselves for happiness. The problem occurs when one expects another human being to make him or her happy. This is your first signal of a co-dependent individual. Co-dependent people will make you feel responsible for their happiness! Those are some pretty big shoes to fill!

When they are not happy it must be your fault! They will start to request for you to change something about yourself. It might be your work, your body, your friends or even your education. This should be your first giant red flag!

A potential mate who is not happy with themselves will project this unhappiness on to you. Many in the early relationship bliss stage are not even yet aware of the change requests. They can be satisfied with the physical aspects of the relationship, so they are more laid-back about the requests.

The problem occurs when the co-dependent person continues with their unhappiness. His/her defense mechanisms prevent that person from realizing it is their own unhappiness and not the new person in the relationship.

Love has many painful reference points in the brain for some people. The primary caregivers of that individual set the stage for that person's entire life. If love was lacking due to emotional and physical needs being unmet then chances are they will carry this on to their adult life.

If you are entering a new relationship then take notice if your new partner keeps recommending for you to change. Love is when we see the best in another individual and we think their faults are cute!

Remember these 5 signs to look out for when entering your next relationship:

1. A person who tends to react rather than respond to events in his or her life.

2. A person who trashes a previous mate is not yet ready for love.

3. A person who has not found her life's passion will expect you to make her happy.

4. A jealous person can never be happy.

5. A person who does not take ownership of his role in his last failed relationship.

Q **What do you not like about yourself?**

A **There is no greater time to be conscious than when one is entering an intimate relationship.** A common trend in America is to rush into a relationship based on physical needs or fears of being alone. Many engage in the musical chairs of dating, quickly picking a mate before the music has stopped.

Everyone is unconscious in some area of their lives. A person's habits are just one example of an unconscious area. The fastest way to increase consciousness in one's mate selection is to pay attention to who is showing up at the door. The relationship you attract is a mirror of how you treat yourself.

Lisa attracted a highly educated good-looking man with a great personality. She really thought this man had potential. Everything was going well until he started pointing out what she needed to change. He first focused on her looks and suggested she drop a few pounds in order to be perfect. Next, he wanted her to get plastic surgery so that she could be truly stunning.

Lisa had attracted the exact same man she had just left. It is no surprise, because no change in her outside world will occur until she changes what occurs in her inside world. You see Lisa was still stuck blaming her ex-husband for being a shallow Hal. She never once contemplated her role in her relationship problems.

If you are attracting what you do not want then it is imperative to observe what is going on. If Lisa chooses to use the power of observation in her favor then she can move past these painful encounters. If Lisa loved herself more she would not be attracting men who insisted on changing her.

Lisa needs to do an inventory on what she does not like about herself. If she fails to recognize what she does not like then she will continue to attract a mate to point out these faults until she learns to love them. Is this man in her life empowering her to learn more self-love? If Lisa was truly satisfied with her physique then she would not be attracting into her life a man who requested such changes.

Conscious dating is when one stops blaming the messenger and uses the skill of observation. Unfortunately, too many people get stuck in blaming the person showing up at the door. Once Lisa learns the skill of observation when dating, then she can recognize what adjustments are necessary to attract a loving relationship. Every mate will be challenging for Lisa until she learns to love herself more.

Love requires consciousness!

Chapter 5

Attraction

Q **How do I raise the caliber of the people I date?**

A **Many people rush into relationships before the ink is dry on their divorce decree.** They bring their prior relationship baggage into the new relationship. Their partner choice is far from who they would pick had they taken the time to heal from their divorce.

Tom joined an online dating site within weeks of filing for divorce. He had his checklist of qualities he desired in a woman. His requirements needed to be that the woman was weight proportionate, employed, drug-free, and childless. Tom met a woman in a few days and within nine weeks they had moved in together. Tom was already discussing marriage on the second date.

Boundaries were clearly lacking with Tom and he met a woman with similar boundary issues. Tom never took the time to heal from his prior relationship. Nor did he take the time to assess his role in his prior failed relationship.

Tom approached a mate like a business decision. He wanted a woman to share expenses with who was also a Republican. His main goal was to get a woman who assisted him in household chores and raising his children.

Julie suffers from co-dependency and has trouble being alone. She lacks conscious awareness and has no clue who has just entered her life. Co-dependent people have a strong need to be needed. She gets her value in life by feeling needed. Co-dependency is often confused with love since Julie grew up in a co-dependent family.

Her subconscious mind thinks "love" is when one feels needed. Love actually requires conscious awareness and not filling in Tom's checklist to not feel alone, doing household chores and babysitting his children.

Co-dependent relationships are a set-up for misery. An unenlightened male might have control issues. An unenlightened female might present drama and emotional unbalance. A co-dependent person does not feel complete being alone. He will assign his happiness to a person outside of himself. This is a recipe for disaster and future litigation.

Co-dependent people rush entirely too soon into relationships with people they barely know. Julie fails to ask questions and believes everything Tom tells her regarding his last two divorces. If your relationship is rushing too fast then chances are you have encountered a co-dependent person.

Many miss the warning signs since the ego is so flattered with all the attention.

Love does not happen overnight. But a co-dependent relationship does!

 Why do I attract emotional vampires?

Emotional vampires can be friends, family members, co-workers, neighbors, or a potential love interest. The problem is one often lacks the clarity as to why one's energy is being drained. It might be attributed to the summer heat, work, stress, family conflict, or a hormonal imbalance. Regardless of the reason it takes a heavy toll on one's health and vitality. The seven reasons below will help prevent you from having your energy drained.

1. You lack appropriate boundaries: A person who is always available is a set up for an emotional vampire. Julie works as an accountant from home. Her fiancé Tom calls non-stop to share his various stresses of his career as a district manager. Julie feels obligated to take his calls because she desires to be in a relationship and detests feeling lonely. In addition, every time Tom calls it gets her off task from completing her upcoming tax deadlines.

2. You have trouble saying no: Julie suffers from an approval addiction and thus fears being rejected by the man she loves. Tom is actually a great guy but who has way more free time on his hands than Julie. In order for Julie to prevent getting her energy drained she needs to up the number of times she says "NO" in her life. She can increase the number of no responses until all of her tax preparations are done for her clients. This action will empower her to actually be a better mate for Tom and less resentful of his frequent phone calls. She will not get stuck in blaming another person for being drained and be able to discontinue the cycle of being taken off task.

3. You are emotionally needy: People who are emotionally needy almost always lack boundaries. Do you have trouble being alone? If so just know you will attract yet another dysfunctional relationship until you learn to be comfortable on your own. Julie jumps into relationships way too soon without giving herself time to heal from her prior relationship. Emotionally needy people gain their self-worth by being needed and valued by others. This altruistic quality will leave any person feeling drained and on the floor.

4. You are afraid to hurt people's feelings: People who are very sensitive often have trouble with potentially hurting others feelings. The problem is Julie is now the one suffering and is paying the price with her depleted energy field. Feelings are a two-way street so Julie needs to consider her own as well.

5. You have a high amount of subconscious guilt: Many
    people are clueless to the long-term consequences of losing
    a loved one. Unresolved grief can leave a person feeling
    like she needs to be the next Mother Theresa in serving
    others. Julie had lost all of her siblings at a young age and
    never connected the dots with her overly helpful behavior.
    The pain of not being able to help a loved one can haunt
    you years later with extreme altruistic behavior. If you find
    yourself always offering to help others but rarely receiving
    help, then it's time to gain some much-needed balance.

    A simple affirmation such as, "Divine spirit, I choose to
    release all guilt and self-sabotage behavior and live in God's
    abundance of love and joyous relationships", is something
    you can repeat 100 times a day. Affirmations are very similar
    to self-hypnosis in that you are programming your own
    subconscious mind by repeating this affirmation out loud.

6. You are not on track with your goals or purpose: Julie
    needed to make a checklist every day to complete what she
    wanted to accomplish. She can gain some much-needed
    structure to not get off task with all of Tom's phone calls.
    Next, before she goes to bed each night she can review
    what behavior interrupted her completing her checklist and
    eliminate the annoying behavior. This will result in Julie
    having more energy and less resentment towards the man
    she loves. Consider creating checklists detailing the positive
    steps you can take to create and accomplish what you really
    want. Don't be afraid to enlist professional help if needed.

7. Co-dependent tendencies: Co-dependent people frequently react in an overly-sensitive manner. "They are often hyper-vigilant to disruption, troubles, or disappointments and remain loyal to people who do not do anything to deserve their loyalty" (Substance Abuse Treatment, 2004). In addition, co-dependent people like Julie dread any form of confrontation, and often do not speak up for what they want in an effort to avoid any unnecessary arguments.

Unfortunately, too many people go through life blaming others for why their energy is being drained.

The truth is you cannot be drained unless you allow it to happen.

Q **What are the signs my girlfriend is a gold digger?**

A **Divorce is truly one of the most painful events in a person's life.** Many men jump right back into a relationship rather than taking the time to heal themselves. The new relationship acts like a Band-Aid and creates a great diversion. This is only a temporary diversion and his pain will resurface again at a later date.

Some men marry right away to hurt their ex-wife. The problem occurs when their radar is off from all their emotional pain. Some men miss some critical warning signals while seeking revenge against their ex-wife. Then others more vengeful will go for one of the wives' friends to really punish her for leaving him.

Here are 5 warning signs the woman you are with does not have your best interest in mind or heart:

1. She is pressuring you to buy a ring and get married. No man needs to be pushed into such a commitment. Especially a man who has yet to heal from a previous divorce.

2. She ignores the fact that your children are in emotional pain and demands all of your attention.

   A woman who truly loves you will love your kids as well. She will know that they too are a part of your life and will encourage you to not ignore your children after a divorce. A gold digger will often only include her own children and do her best to dump yours on your ex-wife. She might never give you any free time to spend one-on-one with your own children.

3. A gold digger will move in and take over your house right away. She might move in her children as well without any consideration of how it impacts your children's mental health. A kind woman would be more concerned about how moving in too soon might impact your children. She would put your kid's needs before her own. She would also encourage you to have a peaceful relationship with your ex-wife for your children's sake.

4. A gold-digger would be taking advantage of the fact that you are in grave emotional pain. She would not encourage you to seek any outside mental health counseling since your unconsciousness aids her planning. She might pay sometimes but do not be fooled if she is not encouraging you to have a relationship with your children. Children often see through a phony person and are the first to notice any inconsistencies.

5. The gold-digger nags you to hurt your ex-wife financially so there is more for her. She goes out of her way to teach you how to screw over your ex-wife in litigation. She might volunteer to help you hide your assets. Any woman who encourages you to hurt the mother of your children is a giant red flag. A kind woman would not inflict pain or add any unnecessary drama to your life.

Look for the woman who puts your children's needs before her own!

Q **Why do I attract gold diggers?**

A **Many men live in intense fear of the opposite sex.** Often times they have paid out a big portion of their net worth to their significant other. Not to mention all the blood-sucking lawyers' extravagant fees and grueling depositions into their private life. After this painful ordeal, many men equate women or committed relationships to extreme pain, thus blocking love from ever entering their life again.

In addition, the extreme levels of anger and resentment can have devastating consequences to one's health. Intense anger can interfere with one's focus, sleep, creativity and one's overall perception. Next, add on rising blood pressure or excess alcohol consumption to self-medicate emotional pain.

A common mistake of many men is to apply this painful event to all women. It is not unusual to see dating self-sabotage after an agonizing divorce.

Unfortunately, many men can remain stuck for years in their anger and resentment. This can result in them not living in present day awareness. They get stuck in the past repeating their story over and over to anyone who will listen. The emotional pain will prevent them from learning the overall life lesson that got them into this situation. The ego can keep them stuck in a victim mentality filled with blame and denial for years. Victims always live with a past sense of awareness.

If he does not get over his victim mentality he runs the risk of repeating this experience again. If one has victim thinking then he will draw in victimizing events into his life.

David went on a date with Julie. He informs her on their first date that his middle name is "cheap". He goes on to say that he will never again get married. Next, he tells Julie, "If you're my partner you better never ask me to buy you any jewelry!"

David then wonders why Julie does not return his phone calls or text messages. He thought he was being very honest about where he stands in a relationship. It is obvious that David has a great deal of anger towards women. His fear of being victimized is making sure no woman ever falls in love with him again. The sad fact was that he actually really enjoyed Julie's company but chased her away with his negative energy.

What David needed to do was process these highly negative emotions. He needed to ask himself what his role was in losing half his assets. It takes two to have a problem so at least analyze your part so you never have to be traumatized again. Perhaps David never showed any respect for his wife. Then again, he might have been unconscious when he picked her in the first place. There are some brutal women out there but just examine your role and get conscious so that you do not make the same mistakes again.

Life is too short to be filled with anger and resentment! Live a life filled with love! You deserve it!

Q **Men ask:**
Why did she blow me off?

A **Have you ever wondered why a woman blew you off?** It seemed as if everything was going great, but she now refuses to answer your texts or phone calls. Women can certainly know what they want right away.

1. Never comment on her body parts or physical attributes. If they look good just know you are about the seventh or eighth man in line noticing that day. This strategy can immediately put a woman on guard to go into protection mode. Statistically, 3 out of 5 women have suffered from some sort of sexual abuse. It is pretty common that prior to that abuse they heard some of those exact same comments. It is always a safer bet to comment on her big brown eyes.

2. Engage her in conversation but refrain from pawing her right away. A woman needs to feel safe, and invading her body space too soon is a great way to make her pull away. It is also a safer bet to meet her at an establishment than to invite her over to your house right away. She will immediately think you are only looking for a hook-up.

3. If your only method of communication is texting just know you will be the first to go when she meets someone who is capable of an actual adult phone conversation. Next, you try to make it a committed relationship too soon. This is just

not normal and chances are she can see through your plan for a quick encounter.

The man that wins the girl does not have to be better looking. He does need to show respect and have integrity. This means talking to her as an individual with a heart and feelings. Be the person who actually cares about her as a person and not just a woman with nice body parts.

Men often forget how much a woman is pursued by the opposite sex.

It is important to not be like the rest so that you stand out.

A man with class and integrity will be chosen over any man with crude or offensive comments.

Chapter 6

Preserve Your Assets the Second Time Around

Q **What is asset protection?**

A **Asset protection is a process and a set of tools used to prevent creditors from successfully attacking your personal assets, business assets, or you.** These creditors can be a person or entity claiming they were harmed in some way, either financially or otherwise. In any event, they are looking to get money or other assets from you!

In this chapter, we are going to focus on a future spouse or significant other as a potential creditor.

We're not saying you should not trust your partner, we're here to educate you. If you are going to get married or enter into a long-term relationship, you want to be aware of potential problems we've come across.

Disclaimers: Asset protection laws are complex, vary from state to state, and typically require legal counsel for effective and legal implementation.

 Who needs asset protection?

 Anyone who has something to lose! If you have very little money, then you don't need to worry about asset protection. If you have cash in the bank, a house with equity in it, jewelry, collectibles, a business, investments, or real estate, then you need to be concerned about creditors. Keep in mind each state varies on how much home equity you can keep from creditors.

Q **What are some of the problems and scams that can occur in marriage, which require asset protection?**

A **Let's address problems first, then scams.**

Problems are those arising unintentionally or unexpectedly from your spouse or significant other. Your spouse may not be specifically trying to harm you, but you could be harmed. Perhaps he or she has significant debt, is behind on child support payments or alimony, has a business that will fail, could be sued, is lousy with money-his/her own and yours, or has an addiction such as gambling or drugs. You may not realize your spouse has a problem. They may not have a problem when you first get together but develop it in the future. Any of these potential issues can be a threat to your money and property.

Scams are frightening, are more common than you might think, and they can be devastating to your finances. Law enforcement is currently seeing a rise in these types of crimes. An example of this could be your spouse/significant other stealing from your accounts without your knowledge.

How could that happen, you might be thinking? Wouldn't I see the money missing from the account? Sure, if you're looking. If your spouse is the one who is handling the finances, you may have no idea what is going on. A cheating spouse may collaborate with a lover to steal your assets, or might be coerced.

Another scam affects the elderly who have cognitive issues, such as dementia or Alzheimer's. Somebody gets close to the victim and convinces them to change beneficiaries or give money to the scammer. It could be a new spouse, significant other, caregiver, or even a child. The first signs of this are often isolation from family and friends. In order to minimize the chances of this happening to you, plan in advance by letting those who will inherit from you know what to expect, ask financial institutions you have accounts with to notify a person of your choosing of any changes in beneficiaries or large withdrawals. Give your financial advisor written authorization to contact someone of your choosing, if they feel something is of concern. Placing some assets in irrevocable trusts can also decrease the chances of this sort of thing from occurring.

Q **Can I protect my assets and my children's assets from my current spouse?**

A **It would be fraudulent to put in place asset protection measures to protect against a current spouse.** If you're single, you can put in place asset protection strategies that can protect you in a future marriage, but not after you're married.

There are some ways to make it more difficult for a spouse to access your money without your permission. Tell the company you have an account with, that in order to access money, the company must confirm your identity by calling your cell number. Some companies may be willing to do this and others not, but it's worth a try. How about stashing some cash away in case of an emergency? If your bank account was drained and your credit cards canceled, at least you would have some money in place while you figure out what happened and go through the process of rebuilding. The amount you'd want to stash away will depend on your income and expenses. This may sound sneaky, but if it protects you from becoming a victim, or limits the damage, it will be well worth it. These measures are especially important if you are not the breadwinner or not working at all, such as a stay-at-home parent.

Q **Finances bore me to death, but my spouse enjoys it.** Do I need to know what we have?

A **Absolutely!** This isn't about having fun. It's making sure you protect yourself, your children and your financial future by spending a little time and effort. It doesn't have to take much time. If your spouse hides his or her assets and leaves you, what are you going to do? Legally they have to disclose everything to you in a divorce. Realistically, he or she may not. By knowing what your spouse has, prior to any indication of a problem, you can use the law to level the playing field if that becomes necessary. You're not trying to take advantage of your spouse, but you don't want to be taken advantage of, either. I've had clients tell me that after 20+ years of marriage, they felt like they had no idea the person who they were married to for all those years could treat them that way.

Q **I have no idea what investments my spouse has.** What can I do about that if they won't tell me?

A **Your tax return is an excellent source.** 1099's, paystubs, etc. are included in your tax returns. Make sure you review them. Tax returns provide a wealth of information on your spouse's financial picture, as well as your own. If you do not know what to look for, ask a financial professional, such as a financial planner, to assist you. Schedule a time to stop by to see your accountant, even if you have never met before.

Look at a pay stub to see what deductions are coming out. That can indicate if your spouse has stock options, a 401(k), a pension plan, and employer or employee paid life insurance. Check files for accounts, if your spouse keeps hard copy files. If you know where the passwords are kept, that could help identify what companies your spouse has accounts with. As a spouse, you have every right to know these things. After all, what if your spouse passed away? Think about the nightmare it would be to get everything squared away if you have no knowledge of what your spouse has. You may keep personal bank account passwords private, but your spouse should either know you have a personal bank account or in the event of your passing away, they should be able to find that out. Perhaps keep the information marked as "Personal" at work so the family will receive that information if a death did occur, when personal effects are returned.

Q **What affect will getting remarried have on my Social Security benefits?**

A **That depends on your age when you remarry and how long your prior marriage(s) lasted.** In order to have the right to receive spousal benefits based upon an ex-spouse, you must have been married at least 10 years (and divorced for at least 2 years, or it's treated as though you are still married). If you remarry before age 60, and stay married, you lose the ability to collect based on your ex-spouses social security. You may collect based upon yours or your new spouse's benefit. The benefit you receive will not affect what your ex-spouse or new spouse receives. If that new marriage ends, then you may be entitled again to a social security benefit based upon your first ex-spouse.

If you remarry after you turn 60, you may qualify for one of the following social security benefits: yours, half of your ex-spouse's benefit, or half of your current spouse's benefit.

In order to actually received social security benefits based upon an ex-spouse, they must be at least 62 years old and you must be at least 62 years old, unless they are deceased, in which case its age 60. If you collect based upon your own benefits, you must be at least 62 years old.

Q When I remarry, how do we merge our money... the smart way?

A **Discuss bills.** Who will pay what? A joint account can be used for paying bills, such as the mortgage, utilities, food, and other expenses. A set amount should be agreed upon and contributed monthly. You can both see this account and know the bills are getting paid. If your spouse isn't paying bills and hasn't told you, you'll discover it much faster in a joint account than if it was supposed to be paid from an individual checking account.

Each of you should also have a separate account. Separate accounts help avoid arguments. Husbands are less likely to gripe about trips to the salon and wives are much less likely to complain about a husband's electronic "toys". Personal expenses such as child support from a previous marriage or alimony can also be paid from these accounts.

Credit cards should be another topic of conversation. Should you have joint credit cards or separate? You've probably figured out the best answer to this one already. Separate credit cards are better. I once spoke with a woman who had a joint credit card and her then husband used it to buy lingerie for his girlfriend. After the divorce, he stopped paying the bills, so she had to pay off all the credit card debt (including the lingerie), in order to avoid destroying her credit. Need I say more?

 How about tax returns? Should we file jointly or separately?

 Most couples will file joint taxes, but there are circumstances where you'll want to file separately. If your spouse has tax troubles, and you file jointly, you may be just as liable for any taxes owed.

Filing separately may have better protections. An example would be if your spouse is a business owner who is, let's just say, aggressive with his or her deductions, and you're concerned about the repercussions of an audit.

One benefit of filing jointly is that you'll have a right to see the tax return, so you can have a better idea what's going on with your spouse's finances.

Whatever you acquire during the marriage is usually going to be considered marital property. Real estate, investments, and cars are examples.

If you inherit property, in many states, it's going to be yours, as long as you keep it "sole and separate property." Keep it separate from any joint assets. If you merge it with joint assets, it's no longer "sole and separate." Prenuptial agreements or trusts may be used to deal with cases like this.

Be sure to consult with a tax professional for any tax matters.

Q **What if my new spouse wants to know my passwords?**

A **Often there is one spouse who takes the lead with finances.** He or she wants to know your passwords and will view your accounts, make legitimate changes, and even change the passwords. With some accounts that is fine. But for accounts specifically under your name, don't share the passwords. This includes your investments and bank accounts in your name only. Sharing the statements is okay, if they are managing the finances, but not your passwords. Unfortunately, there are too many examples where a spouse/significant other will steal or deplete the funds (even after decades of a "happy" marriage). You may think it would never happen to you, but it has happened to numerous people, and is happening more frequently than you think. (Especially if a spouse is planning to divorce.)

Q How important is it to discuss finances with my significant other?

A Not only is it important to discuss finances prior to getting married or moving into a long-term relationship, but it's also important to keep the lines of financial communication open throughout the relationship. As a financial planner, I regularly review my client's accounts and their goals with them face-to-face. You can do the same with your partner. Are you spending too much? Saving enough? If you're thinking about making a big purchase, you should talk it over together. The last thing you want is your spouse surprising you by coming home with a new car or piece of jewelry that you cannot afford, then saying, "We don't have enough money to save like we wanted to for retirement." The goal is to reduce severe money arguments.

Q When should we discuss our finances (and credit scores)?

A The first step is to have a detailed conversation about your finances prior to marriage — well in advance. I recommend you have that talk if you are discussing getting married or soon after getting engaged. If there are any red flags, you want to become aware of them as soon as possible.

What if your soon-to-be spouse refuses to discuss his or her finances with you? Tell your fiancé that after having gone through marriage/divorce once, you've learned that it is vital to a successful marriage to discuss finances before making a commitment.

You may wonder why I mention credit scores. Who talks about credit scores unless you're buying a house or car? Presumably, at some point you will buy a car, house, refinance, apply for a credit card, apply for a job, or any other big ticket or important step, which will rely on your credit score. If your spouse has a low score, it may require you to cosign, leaving you responsible and a default could cause you problems. Again, the more information you have up front, the better prepared you are to make good decisions about your financial future. It may not be easy to have these conversations, but they are extremely important.

I have a trust. That will protect my assets from future spouses and creditors, right?

The most common form of a trust is the revocable living trust. The key word here is revocable. A revocable trust is not going to protect your assets from future spouses and creditors. These trusts do have some benefits, but not asset protection. In case of divorce, or if a creditor brings a case to court, you could be ordered to remove the assets from the trust. Irrevocable trusts are much better suited for asset protection.

Q **My new partner says they're good with finances.** Should I let my partner handle mine?

A **Its true, often one of the people in the relationship does not like to handle finances.** Unfortunately, a dishonest partner can take advantage. If you're not married and are in a newer relationship, it is in your best interest not to allow access to any of your accounts. It is best to use a financial planner who works for you. If your partner keeps asking you to disclose your finances and wants to manage them for you, it can be a red flag. It may be that the person has control issues, or perhaps he or she has criminal motives. Sad as it is, people do steal from their partners.

This is not limited to new couples, crime happens in long-term relationships, as well. For example, if one spouse plans to divorce and steals from the other spouse's accounts. There have even been cases, where the dishonest spouse had solicited the new mate to pretend to be the account owner, in order to gain access to the money.

It is a good idea to keep a bank account that is yours, and completely separate from your spouse. No password sharing, no statement sharing. It's your safety net in case your other accounts are compromised. You may need that money to cover living expenses and attorney fees.

I'm concerned that if either of us gets sued for anything, all our money is at risk. Can I get insurance for that?

It depends on what you are being sued for. If what you did was intentionally harmful, then no insurance will help you.

Assuming any harm caused by your action or inaction was unintentional, then there is insurance to help add a layer of protection. If you have any assets worth suing for, or will in the future, then I highly recommend purchasing umbrella liability insurance for non-work related issues. This type of insurance helps cover the judgment and/or attorney's fees in addition to the maximum amounts provided by your auto and homeowners insurance. Typically sold in million-dollar increments, it is very affordable, assuming you shop it around. You can purchase it from your home and auto insurance company. Examples of where this type of insurance could come in handy are, if you're in a car accident and your auto insurance maximum payout is $350,000, but the judgment against you is $1,000,000. Rather than leaving you to pay out of pocket up to the remaining $650,000, the umbrella liability policy pays the amount. It may not be you, but could be your spouse or minor child who caused the accident. Let's say a neighborhood child gets hurt in your yard -- it works the same way. This type of insurance coverage is not limited to incidents involving your car or home.

What is important to remember here is that it is for non-work-related problems. There is separate insurance for business-related liability. That is very important to have as well! Insurance alone is not enough to protect your assets. It's simply one more layer of protection.

Q **Are there investments that have creditor protection?**

A **Traditional investments, such as stocks, bonds, mutual funds, etc.,** do not have creditor protection. They would have to be owned outside of the person's estate, such as by an irrevocable trust, in order to accomplish that goal. There are vehicles that can assist in protecting your money from creditors, depending on which state you live in.

Annuities may provide protection from creditors. Some states allow unlimited amounts to be creditor protected, other states allow a set amount, and some states do not allow any to be exempt from creditors. Some states have a waiting period—a length of time for how long you must own the annuity prior to it being protected. As of the date of this book's publication, my state of residence, Arizona, allows for 100% creditor protection as long as the annuity has been in place at least two years, the beneficiaries are family members, and there is no current creditor problem, nor are any anticipated.

Because the laws change, we are not including a state-by-state run-down in this book. Be sure to check with an attorney for your individual state.

Life insurance policies with cash value may have creditor protection as well. The rules of any individual state may be the same for life insurance as with annuities, or different. Arizona happens to be the same for both.

Q **Should my spouse be a co-owner of the business?**

A **If your spouse is not actively engaged in the business, then it may not be a good idea for him or her to be an owner.** If creditors come after your spouse, and he or she is an owner of the business, that may potentially subject the business to the claims of those creditors.

Q **What can happen to us if my child were to get into a serious car accident?**

A **If your child is involved in a serious auto accident or something similar, and injures, disables, or kills someone, and your child is a minor, your assets may be at risk.** It is like any other creditor coming after your assets. Once you are sued, it is too late to protect your assets. That would not be legal. The planning must be done ahead of time.

Various ways to help reduce your exposure to creditors can include insurance, (auto, home, and umbrella), titling assets that are business-related in the name of the business and not in your name, certain kinds of trusts, LLC's, cash value life insurance/ annuities (in some states), avoiding co-signing loans, etc. These are important to have because judgments can easily exceed the amount of auto or homeowners insurance coverage you have. You are not necessarily trying to avoid paying, but instead, get creditors to negotiate a much lower settlement.

Chapter 7

The Financially Irresponsible Future Spouse

Q How do I find out if my significant other has a serious mental health condition since it's not always obvious while dating?

A **This may seem like a strange question to ask, but it is very important to know the answer prior to marriage.** Could your future spouse be bipolar, have anger issues, or depression, etc. I know someone who was in a marriage like this because he had no idea during the dating process, that his significant other had serious mental health problems. Regardless of what you choose to do with that information (perhaps nothing or possibly end the relationship, for example), you want to be aware of it ahead of your wedding.

The straightforward, and healthiest, approach is simply to ask. Obviously, I would advise against asking this on a first date! But, as the relationship evolves, you have every right to want to know what health issues your significant other has. A relationship is built on trust, having a discussion will likely help both parties.

If you suspect the person you're dating has serious mental health issues, but are not ready to discuss them, the least confrontational approach is to look in the medicine cabinet and see what the person takes (or should be taking). Write down the name and dosage of the medication and research what it typically treats. This may give you a clue, but beware that medications could have many uses and can be prescribed for different conditions, so do not assume. Sounds like an invasion of privacy, doesn't it? Well, yes it is. Do you want to know what problems the person has or don't you?

Not only is mental health important, but so is physical health. Your partner may not always be honest with what health issues they have. One way to check if your partner is not telling you something important is to check the last few pages of their life or disability insurance policies. If your partner has applied for life, disability, or health insurance, then he or she would have had to disclose their health information during the application process. Life and disability insurance policies should have a copy of that information toward the back of the policy.

So how does this tie back to a financially irresponsible spouse? If your spouse, or future spouse, has serious mental health issues, this can make them a threat to their money and potentially your money. It's possible they could have out of control spending habits (due to something like a gambling addiction), need expensive medical treatments, or other types of rehabilitation. These are all things you should know about, so you can protect yourself and your spouse.

Q **I love my fiancé, but he/she has an addiction.** I want to protect myself, my children, and my assets. What can I do to accomplish that?

A **Unfortunately, addictions are all too common.** Common addictions include gambling, sex, drugs, alcohol and many others. The threat to your family and financial situation is real. This chapter will address the threat to your assets. (The next chapter will discuss protecting yourself and your children.)

The primary way to prevent your assets from being taken by the addict is to prevent them from having access to your money. Keep in mind, an addict is not necessarily going to follow the law. Close joint bank accounts. Keep passwords to accounts, and your financial information of all sorts away from the house. Store them in your office or bank safe deposit box. Tell your financial institutions you want an extra security measure put in place and explain the situation. They may be able to accommodate that. Close home equity and personal lines of credit to future withdrawals or require both parties to sign. Freeze your credit. Notify credit agencies that you want to opt out of prescreened credit offers. Go to optoutprescreen.com. Use a service that notifies you if anyone opens up a line of credit in your name. If your significant other lives with you, have your financial mail/e-mail go to a separate account that you don't access from your home computer. Remove anything that the person might pawn, such as valuable jewelry and collectibles.

If you marry the person, then the measures described above will still help, but they are not enough. Keep as many of your assets as sole and separate property as you can. As stated previously, do not commingle the assets, or you'll lose the sole and separate property status. Check their pay stub to make sure they are still having the appropriate amount of taxes being withheld and have not canceled insurance or other benefits. You do not want a surprise tax bill next year! You may want to change the title on your large assets such as cars, boats, house, so your addict spouse cannot use them as collateral for loans. It may also be beneficial to file your tax return separately if your spouse has done anything that could cause problems with the IRS. You do not want to be responsible for extra taxes and penalties!

Depending on how much you have in the way of assets to protect, you may create a trust with spendthrift provisions. There are some downsides to doing this, but depending on the severity of the problem, it may be beneficial.

My fiancé spends money like there is an endless supply of it. What can I do short of ending the relationship?

A number of the recommendations from the previous question are applicable here, as well. The important point is that you restrict access to your money by your future spouse. In addition, consider creating an asset protection trust to hold some assets prior to marriage. This can give added protection because a trustee has control of the assets, not you or your spouse, so they cannot withdraw funds at will to support a spendthrift lifestyle.

Notice the question reads fiancé. Once you're married, it's too late to move your assets to a trust to protect them from your spouse. This has to be done in advance.

Chapter 8

Unmarried Couples and Their Finances, Let's Get it Right!

Q **Does our state consider us married, even though we are not?**

A **Some states have common law marriage.** If your state is one of them, then you may be considered married by that state, and some cities. If you do not reside in one of those states, or do not meet the qualifications that the state lists, then they do not consider you to be married. If you are living with someone, this does not automatically establish a common law marriage, even in a common law marriage state. Requirements for a common law marriage in states that allow for it, typically include the following: You must live together, have the intent to be married, hold yourself out to friends and family as being married, have joint bank/credit card accounts, be of a certain age (varies by state), have the capacity to marry, and be of sound mind.

Each of the states with common law marriage have their own rules. In 2017, the list of states that currently have it on the books include Colorado, District of Columbia, Iowa, Kansas, New Hampshire, Montana, Rhode Island, South Carolina and Texas. Utah does not recognize common law marriage but can retroactively approve the marriage of couples without ceremony if they meet certain requirements. Several other states no longer have the law on the books, but recognize common law marriages prior to the law being abolished. Those states include Florida, Georgia, Idaho, Indiana, Ohio, Oklahoma, Pennsylvania and Alabama. Marriage laws may change, so check with a family law attorney in your state.

 What are the different kinds of unmarried couples and what are the differences between them?

 These include registered domestic partners, unregistered domestic partners and civil unions.

Registered domestic partners are not considered married, but are a formal relationship, that must meet certain qualifications. The IRS does not consider them as married for tax purposes. A small number of states and some cities recognize them as well as some employers for purposes of benefits. They give some of the benefits of marriage, such as insurance benefits and basic visitation rights, but on the negative side, may add financial liability for the partner's debts, and may lack portability of benefits from an employer.

Unregistered domestic partners have no official benefits, but have none of the legal drawbacks either.

Civil unions are also a formal relationship that, like domestic partnerships, provide legal rights that are similar to marriage. A small number of states still have them. Some states converted civil unions to marriage when same-sex marriage became legal in all states in 2015. The benefits vary with each state that offers them. They do not have federal benefits. They may not transfer to other states.

 What would happen if I'm unmarried and my partner was suddenly hospitalized or became disabled?

 In most states, an unmarried couple does not have the same rights as a married couple with regard to medical decisions, unless you have planned ahead of time.

Suppose Doug was in a car accident and was rushed to the hospital. You're his partner, but not married. If he cannot communicate, then you may have no decision-making rights regarding Doug. His family members may determine if he remains on life-support. In order to minimize the chances of this occurring, you both should have healthcare and mental health powers of attorney created. Many hospitals require them to be updated frequently. You'll want to keep it handy, perhaps as an attachment in an email or have a copy in your car, in addition to keeping a copy in your home. It's helpful if a loved one has a copy as well, especially if you're a senior and more prone to hospital visits.

There can be benefits to being unmarried and in a relationship. If your partner needs to spend down their assets to pay for long-term care, in order to qualify for Medicaid benefits, your assets will not need to be factored in. A married couple would have their total assets taken into account in order to qualify for benefits.

Q **Will my partner receive health insurance from my employer while I'm still working?**

A **A domestic partner may be eligible for health insurance benefits from your employer.** Only one state, California, at the time of this book's publication, requires that an employer offer domestic partner health insurance benefits to employees, as part of their health insurance plan. In 2016, approximately 41% of employers surveyed (by the International Foundation of Employee Benefit Plans) offered domestic partner benefits to all employees and 48% offered them only to same-sex couples. According to surveys, these numbers may decrease since same-sex couples are now allowed to marry. It is surprising more do not offer domestic partner health insurance benefits, considering 7.5 million unmarried couples live together in the U.S., according to the 2010 U.S. Census data.

Even if an employer's health insurance plan includes domestic partner health insurance benefits, they are generally not tax-friendly. Health insurance premiums paid by the employer for the employee's domestic partner are usually taxable to the employee as earned income on their W-2. If the partner is a spouse, the premiums are not taxable.

Q **Will getting remarried affect my future social security payments?**

A **It might.** There are two scenarios to consider: divorced with a living ex-spouse and widowed. If you are divorced, were married for at least 10 years, and your spouse paid into social security for at least 10 years, and you did not remarry before you turn age 60, then you qualify for the greater of either half of your spouse's social security benefit or your own full benefit. If you remarry before age 60, you lose the ability to receive half of your ex-spouses benefit. If your ex earned significantly more than you and more than your new spouse, getting remarried can make a difference of thousands of dollars per year for life.

When determining how much you will qualify to receive in future social security benefits, based upon your own earnings, alimony received does not count towards your earnings. If you earn $20,000 from your job this year, and receive $20,000 in alimony this year, only the $20,000 in income from your job counts towards your earnings for your future social security benefits. Child support does not count either.

If you become widowed before you reach your full social security retirement age (66-67 for most people), did not remarry before age 60 (50 if you're disabled), you can receive benefits based upon your deceased ex-spouses full social security earning record, even if your ex had remarried. You can remarry after age 60 and still qualify to receive benefits based on your ex-spouses earnings record. However, if you remarry before age 60, you will not qualify for survivors benefits. You should consider your financial situation carefully as these options can make a significant difference in your income, and may provide an incentive not to remarry.

Q **Will getting remarried affect my current social security payments?**

A **For some people, it may.** If you are divorced, receiving social security benefits from your ex' earning record (as opposed to your own), and remarry, you will no longer be eligible to use your ex-spouse's earning record for your social security benefits, unless your new spouse is also entitled to use their ex-spouse or their deceased spouse's earning record. Depending on the situation, that may result in a significant decrease of social security payments. For many people, social security is a large portion of their overall income, so consider this prior to remarrying. If this new marriage ends, you will qualify for benefits based upon your ex-spouse again.

A divorced person over 60, who remarries, but is not receiving benefits from an ex-spouse's earnings record will not see an impact on their social security payment.

You may qualify to use your new spouse's earnings record to enhance your social security income once you have been married for one year or longer. This assumes your new spouses' benefit is more than double your benefit.

If a person receives Supplemental Security Income (for extremely low-income seniors), remarrying may cause that income to change, based on your spouse's income and assets.

Q **As an unmarried couple, what kind of issues can arise in our 401(k)s, IRAs and other retirement savings plans?**

A **Qualified plans that fall under the Employee Retirement Income Security Act of 1974 (ERISA) guidelines, such as 401(k) and private sector defined benefit pension plans require that a spouse be a beneficiary on the account unless the spouse opts out in writing.** Unmarried domestic partners do not have that automatic protection with these retirement plans. They can certainly be listed as a beneficiary, but it is not automatic. The account owner must designate the domestic partner, in order for them to be the primary beneficiary. Sounds easy enough, but in many cases, people do not update their beneficiaries after entering a serious relationship or ending one. I recall looking over a client's beneficiaries and calling the client to confirm them. When I mentioned the name of her primary beneficiary on her account, who was an ex-boyfriend of hers, she began to panic and emphasized the need to change her beneficiary immediately. Don't let this happen to you…re-evaluate your beneficiaries whenever your relationship or family status changes!

IRA, Roth IRA, and most 403(b) (Non-ERISA) retirement plans typically do not require the spouse to be a beneficiary on the account, however some plans may require a spouse to be a primary beneficiary, especially in community property states. Community property states include Arizona, California, Idaho, Louisiana, Nevada, New Mexico, Texas, Washington and Wisconsin. Alaska allows couples to write a contract to elect some or all of their property to be community property, but it is not mandatory. The beneficiaries are whomever the owner designated most recently. The spouse, if in a community property state, can opt out of these as well by signing the spousal consent section of the beneficiary form. Beneficiary designations supersede a will or trust, so make sure you review with your partner who your beneficiaries are on these types of accounts.

Q **What is the "marriage penalty" I've heard about, and will it affect us if we get married?**

A **The "marriage penalty" is how some people refer to the higher rate of federal income taxation of a married couple than an unmarried couple, assuming each couple has the same earned income.** Based on recent tax-law changes, this now applies only to high-income earners in the upper tax brackets of 35% and 37%.

For example, let's say Karen earns $400,000 and Tim earns $200,000. If they are not married, her top tax bracket is 35%, but his is 32%. If they are married their combined tax bracket is 35% (based upon 2020 tax rates and their combined $600,000 income. We should keep in mind that only a portion of their income is taxed at the top rate, not all of it. The difference in this example is $7,350. If a married couple's combined top tax bracket is below 35%, they will not have a "marriage penalty."

Some couples may experience the opposite effect and could actually reduce their taxes if married (called a marriage bonus). Say, Karen earns $100,000 and Tim earns $50,000. Her tax bracket as a single person is 24%. If they are married, and file jointly, their combined income would put them in the 22% tax bracket. The savings is minimal, but it is better than being penalized.

Q **Do unmarried couples receive the same tax benefits from inheritances as married couples?**

A **They do not.** Married couples are allowed to transfer an unlimited amount of assets to each other without gift or estate taxes. Unmarried couples do not receive the same benefit. This means you can't pass assets of unlimited amount to a partner while alive or upon your death without filing a gift tax/estate tax return and possibly needing to pay gift/ estate taxes. Under current laws, paying gift/estate taxes only impacts the very wealthy, but for those people it can have a substantial impact.

In community property states (Arizona, California, Idaho, Louisiana, Nevada, New Mexico, Texas, Washington and Wisconsin, as of 2020), the death of a spouse would allow a step-up in cost basis of both the deceased spouse and the surviving spouse's portion of jointly owned assets, which reduces capital gains taxes.

Cost Basis is what was paid for an asset and any money put into that asset during the ownership period. An example is a rental home purchased by the deceased and their spouse for $200,000, plus improvements to the house amounting to $15,000, which were made over time. The cost basis is $215,000. A step-up in cost basis means the cost basis of the deceased persons assets change to equal the value on the date of death, which in this example is $400,000. No taxes from the inheritance of the home will be owed by the estate of the deceased. If the couple lived in a non-community property state, half the value would receive a step-up in cost basis.

Unmarried couples do not receive this benefit, regardless of which community property state they live in, because the federal taxes are based upon federal law, not state law. Therefore, only the deceased partner's share gets a step-up in basis, not the surviving partner's. This affects middle-income tax-payers as well as the wealthy.

Is there a limit to how much I can gift my partner, without owing taxes on the gift?

 Yes, there is a limit. As of the date of the publication, there are two amounts one can gift without it being taxable.

First, you can gift $15,000 per year to anyone you choose. For example, let's say Fred has a partner, one child and two grandchildren. He is allowed to gift each of them $15,000 per year, for a total of $60,000 per year.

Second, in addition to the $15,000 per year, you may gift a lifetime amount of $11.58 million. An example of this is Sheila. She gifts $15,000 to five people each year, that's $75,000 per year. This year she also gifted a house worth $500,000 to one of those 5 people. Her lifetime gift exemption amount will drop to $11.08 million. The lifetime gift exemption amount is indexed to increase each year, so that figure will rise. The $15,000 she gifted to five people does not get included in the lifetime gift exemption amount.

Clearly, most people will not be taxed upon amounts gifted to others, but a very small percentage will be. High-net worth people who may owe estate taxes in the future, can use gifting to reduce those taxes, among other methods. Married couples can benefit from gifting unlimited amounts to their spouse, via the marital exemption.

An exception is a non-citizen (and non-resident alien) spouse. If you gift to a non-citizen spouse, the lifetime exemption is $157,000 (as of 2020).

Please note that if you are considering gifting a sizable amount you should check the most current figures. The gifting exemption amounts are a politically charged subject susceptible to change.

Q **What are estate taxes (a.k.a.** "the death tax") and how does it affect us?

A **Estate taxes are a federal or state tax on the value of one's assets at the time of death.** Those assets, which include everything you own, regardless of how much the value is, are called your "estate". Most of us think that in order to have an estate, you need to be wealthy. That is not true, according to federal and state law. Estate sizes will vary tremendously based upon a person's assets.

Most people who pass away in 2020 will not have to pay federal estate taxes because only estates of over $11.58 million (as of 2020) for a single person will be required to pay. (The non-resident alien estate tax exemption is $60,000 in 2020.)

If a person is married, the survivor may utilize the marital exemption and not have to pay any estate taxes on that money until they pass away. It is not automatic, however, and must be elected on the first spouse's estate tax form. As you can tell, very few estates will be subject to federal estate taxes. In reality, about 2/10ths of one percent of the population has an estate large enough to pay federal estate taxes. A spouse who is not a U.S. citizen does not receive the marital exemption. Unlike with gifting, resident aliens do not receive the marital exemption regarding estate taxes. Let's look at an example. If Riley is a U.S. citizen, but his wife Anita is a resident alien, then if Riley passes first, only his assets exceeding the estate tax exemption amount will be taxed. If Anita passes first, none of her estate is taxed, as Riley is a U.S. citizen and can use the marital exemption. There are a couple of types of trusts that may be used to get the marital deduction.

As we've already mentioned, unmarried couples do not get the marital exemption. This means couples who are not married can receive an $11.58 million exemption each, but cannot pass their unused exemption to their partner. For those who have estates of that size, or will in the future, it is very important to plan for how those taxes will be paid. The tax is 40% of the amount over the exemption.

Unlike the federal estate tax described above, the asset amounts required to trigger state estate taxes is frequently much lower than at the federal level. Not every state has estate taxes. Those that do include Connecticut, Delaware, Hawaii, Illinois, Maine, Maryland, Massachusetts, Minnesota, New Jersey, New York, Oregon, Rhode Island, Vermont, Washington D.C. and Washington state. Of those states, Maryland and New Jersey also have an inheritance tax. Four other states have an inheritance tax, but no estate tax. They include Iowa, Kentucky, Nebraska, and Pennsylvania. An inheritance tax is a tax on the value of what you inherit. State estate taxes and inheritance taxes have a marital exemption, but not for unmarried couples.

There are a variety of techniques used to pay for or decrease federal and state estate taxes as well as state inheritance taxes. They include gifting, trusts, and other estate planning techniques. It is extremely important to work with professionals when attempting to reduce estate taxes. The wrong move(s) can be quite costly and problematic for the family. The most notable examples are when a celebrity dies without having planned properly. Family members frequently argue, may have to sell prized assets to pay for taxes, and so on. A former owner of the Miami Dolphins football team died without having planned for estate taxes, and the family had to sell the team. Prince passed away without a will or a trust, leaving state law and a judge in charge of what happens to the estate.

Q **Will I inherit from my partner if he/she passes away before I do?**

A **Not automatically.** Unlike a spouse, if your domestic partner passes away, most state laws do not entitle you to receive an inheritance. Therefore, you both should have in writing what you want to leave to your partner, as well as to anyone else. Methods of doing this include a trust, will, beneficiary paperwork, and certain titling of assets, such as joint tenancy, for example. Married couples should have this as well, but it's even more important that domestic partners have their arrangements in place. If there are no arrangements in place, then state laws typically require the assets of the deceased to go to their relatives, not their domestic partners. Several states have a different set of rules for registered domestic partners/civil unions, giving some of the same benefits as married partners. They include California (same sex or one is age 62+), Washington DC, Maine, Nevada and Oregon (same sex only) have domestic partnership laws. Illinois has a civil union law granting the same benefits to domestic partners as to married partners. Washington has a domestic partnership law for couples where at least one is age 62+. Laws allowing domestic partnerships for those age 62+ is to protect those individuals who could lose social security or pension benefits if they remarry. Keep in mind that state and federal laws change, so do not rely only on the information contained in this answer.

It is all too common for people not to have their documents in order when they die, especially when their passing occurs rapidly. But not having these documents in place can mean a financial disaster for the surviving partner, if he/she is relying on those assets (things like bank accounts, investments, and of course the house) and they go to someone else. Domestic partners frequently want their partner to receive those assets instead of their family receiving the inheritance first. If these are your wishes, then do not procrastinate—get your estate planning documents done!

Do not forget to factor in whoever else you want to inherit the remainder of your assets after the surviving partner passes away. If you pass away first then your partner may, upon their death, leave your assets to a beneficiary of their choice, instead of yours.

Let's look at an example. Tina and Cliff are an unmarried couple. They each have their own assets. They have the proper paperwork in place ensuring when one of them passes away, the other has use of the assets. Cliff passed away first. He wanted Tina to have use of the house, which belonged to him, as well as access to his money. Cliff also has a nephew. He wanted any remaining money left over after Tina dies, along with the house, to go to his nephew. Without proper documentation, Tina could decide to pass those assets to her family, excluding Cliff's nephew. Do not leave your estate to chance!

Q **I want my partner to be taken care of if I die first, but I don't want their family or mine to inherit the money after my partner passes.** How can I accomplish this?

A **It can be accomplished through the use of a trust.** The language should state what the primary beneficiary will receive or be eligible to receive, and that they should not own the assets from the trust. This will ensure the beneficiary does not inherit the assets. If there was no trust, then the beneficiary will designate who receives the remainder after they pass away.

Chapter 9

Prenuptial Agreements

Q **What is a prenuptial agreement?**

A **A prenuptial agreement is a contract between a couple prior to marrying, that details how their assets will be distributed if they get divorced or upon death.**

Q **Do prenuptial agreements really work?**

A **Yes, if properly written and set up.** Here are some requirements of a valid prenuptial agreement:

- Both parties fully disclose their assets…all of their assets.

- It is signed well in advance of the wedding. A pressure situation shortly before the wedding will likely nullify the agreement.

- It should not leave one party destitute.

- Make it a formal agreement, legally bound — not handwritten on a sheet of paper.

- Each of you should have your own attorney knowledgeable in these agreements.

- Both parties need to notarize it.

 I'm getting remarried. Should I get a prenuptial agreement?

 That really depends on the two of you. For some people, they are necessary.

As unromantic as they are, prenuptial agreements do serve a purpose in certain situations. At the very least, have a conversation well ahead of getting married about your finances including debts, and what you want to happen if you divorced or died. There are some situations where a prenuptial agreement can make a lot of sense, such as a second marriage where there are children from the first marriage. The prenuptial helps direct what assets go to your children. Without it, the children may not receive what you want them to. This does not take the place of proper estate planning.

Consider the following to determine if you may benefit from a prenuptial agreement:

1. One of you has significantly more assets than the other. This is a common reason for a prenup; especially if you lost a lot of money in your divorce from a prior marriage.

2. You have assets you absolutely want to remain in your family.

3. One of you has a large amount of debt. If you are marrying someone who has accumulated significant consumer debt, such as on credit cards, it may be in your best interest to have an agreement say that it is not your responsibility. Without that, you can be on the hook for the debt, even if you divorce. Some states, particularly community property states, may provide some protection for pre-existing debt that was brought into the marriage. Seek counsel to make sure you understand the rules in your state.

4. One of you owns a business. The owner wants to protect her livelihood from being co-owned by an ex-spouse or having to come up with ½ the value of the business, to pay off the spouse. You can imagine the problems either scenario brings. On the other hand, the non-owner may not want the liability of being a co-owner if the business does poorly and has a lot of debts. He would be responsible just like the spouse who is the owner. If you have a partner in your business, that further complicates the matter and makes it more beneficial to have a prenuptial agreement. There should

be an agreement with the owners about what happens to the shares if an owner divorces or dies.

5. You have loved ones who need to be taken care of, such as elderly parents. If you lose a significant amount of your assets in a divorce, your family member may not receive the level of care you want him or her to have.

6. One of you will be supporting the other through college. Not a problem if the two of you will be together for the long term, but quite frustrating if you split up shortly after the completion of the degree and you never see the benefit of that degree.

7. Inheritances can be kept separate without a prenup, except if they are commingled with joint assets. A prenuptial agreement can help clarify who gets what. A house you inherited, yet you both live in is a prime example of this.

If you fall into any of these categories it does not mean you must enter into a premarital agreement, but you should consider it. Speak with your financial professionals, including your attorney, financial advisor, and accountant. Perhaps you lost a significant amount of assets in a divorce. Do you want to risk that happening again?

 How do I bring up to my significant other or fiancé that I want a prenuptial agreement?
I don't want to damage or destroy my relationship.

A Starting a conversation about a prenuptial agreement can be extremely difficult, but if you have a good reason for wanting one, then it makes the conversation easier to have.

If you have been through a bad situation where you lost a significant amount of assets due to a divorce or scam from a prior marriage, then you may have a strong argument for wanting a prenuptial agreement. However…if in a prior marriage, you were married since you were young adults and your spouse was a stay-at-home parent, sacrificing their career, then you should expect to have split the assets equitably. Remember, they lost assets by not working. Obviously emotions run high with this topic, and many variables can affect advice, but again, be reasonable and think about it from your partner's perspective as well as your own. This is not about taking advantage of the other person, but about protecting what you have/will have, if the marriage does not work out.

You want to get to know your future spouse's opinions on these subjects soon enough to be able to avoid problems during the marriage. If you cannot talk about sensitive topics like this, it does not bode well for your marriage. Preferably the conversation will occur prior to or soon after getting engaged. Find a neutral, comfortable, relatively quiet place to have this conversation. Not in a restaurant, coffee shop, or other public place. You don't need someone sitting at the next table chiming in with his or her opinion!

State your specific concerns, but be open, honest, and direct. Let it be a discussion, not a one-sided lecture. Work out any issues together and don't be overbearing. Do not wait until the wedding is upon you.

Keeping some property separate can be a good idea for asset protection. If a lawsuit or bankruptcy occurs with one of you, the partners separate assets may be less at risk.

Here are a few conversation starters:

"I believe that marriage is a 50-50 proposition, and I'm concerned about giving up my job to become a full-time stay-at-home spouse. Can we establish a principle of 50-50 sharing at the outset?"

"Let's talk about our future, what we both want, our lifestyles, and our present and future finances. I want to make sure all our money issues are addressed and resolved in an agreement. Then we won't have them hanging over us when we get married."

"One thing I have to consider before we get married is my parents' business. I need to be confident that the business will remain in the family in the event the unthinkable occurs."

 My fiancé wants a prenuptial agreement, but I don't. What should I say?

 It's likely to take an emotional toll on both of you, so approach it rationally.

The first thought is, why does your fiancé want one? Let your partner explain. Does it make sense? Are you going to be hurt financially by it? Will it protect both of you? If it's one-sided and not for a legitimate reason, then you probably will not want to sign it. Explain your position. If your significant other will not have a rational discussion while your relationship is going well, then what will happen when things are not working out? The point is, have the discussion early on. Make sure to have an attorney, financial advisor, and accountant review the document prior to agreeing on anything, and definitely prior to signing it. Your partner should not be taking advantage of you with the agreement. Also, know that an agreement can be structured to end after a period of time, such as 5 years.

 Are there alternatives to prenuptial agreements?

 There are a couple of methods to keep assets protected from future ex-spouses, but they will not completely replace a prenuptial agreement.

Domestic or Foreign Asset Protection Trusts can be very useful for all kinds of creditor protection. These trusts must be set up prior to any creditor issues or expected creditor issues, and must meet any applicable state/federal/international laws. It must be established prior to the marriage to be effective for future ex-spouse creditor protection. A primary benefit of this type of trust is that it protects your assets that are placed in the trust from creditors, including future ex-spouses. Keep in mind that we are talking about a legitimate use of a trust. It will not protect against circumstances of a criminal/illegal nature. The trust can be set up to allow for the creator of the trust to access money during his or her life, at the discretion of the trustee. A few requirements of the trust are that it must be irrevocable, unchangeable, have a spendthrift clause, and appoint a local trustee, corporate or individual. Foreign asset protection trusts can be rather expensive.

Keeping assets you had prior to the marriage as sole and separate property can be an effective way of holding on to those assets if you divorce. As long as you do not co-mingle that property with any joint assets, then you should be fine. If the asset is a house you live in, then it will be much more difficult to keep that as sole and separate because chances are that your spouse will spend money on the house, repairs, etc. That will likely muddy the water in your claim that it was your house, and not subject to being split.

 Can Prenuptial Agreements be changed?

 They can. Both parties must agree and sign the amendments.

An example of a change would be if you owned a house prior to marriage (separate from your primary residence), and it was kept as sole and separate property, listed as such in the prenuptial agreement. After many years of marriage, you want your spouse to have the home. You both could amend the prenuptial agreement to allow for that. An attorney would be used to create the addendum.

Q **Does a Prenuptial Agreement provide for me if my new spouse dies before me?**

A **Many of them do not have well thought out provisions if one spouse passes away and that can be a problem.**

Imagine if you're the survivor, and your spouse, who had the majority of the assets, doesn't provide for you in the prenuptial agreement or trust. In case of their death, the assets go to their children from a prior marriage or perhaps other relatives. It's not unheard of for the children of the late spouse to give the second wife/husband the boot out of the house, once they inherit it. Make sure you address this possibility when discussing the prenuptial agreement, and who gets what when either spouse dies. If it's not in writing, assume it will not happen.

Q **Do I need a prenuptial agreement if I'm in a long-term relationship, but not married?**

A **If you are in a Common Law Marriage state, depending on your circumstances, it may make sense to have a prenuptial agreement, just like with a traditional marriage.** It should be put in place prior to when the Common Law Marriage goes into effect.

Creating a domestic partnership agreement would assist in setting a date for the common law marriage. Splitting-up does not end a Common Law Marriage. Divorce would need to occur to end the marriage. Marriage laws change frequently, so check with a family law attorney in your state.

Q **Will a prenuptial agreement protect my assets from Medicaid's spend-down requirements if my future spouse needs to receive benefits from Medicaid?**

A **In order to qualify for Medicaid (a state-managed government social healthcare program for people with limited resources), a person or couple may need to spend down their non-exempt assets to a minimal amount (as discussed in the chapter on Long Term Care).** Having a prenuptial agreement will not protect any assets from the spend-down requirement.

Chapter 10

How To Make Sure Your Loved Ones Are Protected

 What do I need to know about life insurance?

 You may be thinking that life insurance is morbid and boring, and do we really need to go over this?

Yes…sure do! Here's why. First of all, no one likes insurance, until you need it. The subtitle of this book includes How to Protect Yourself, Your Children, and Your Assets. Life insurance is used in a variety of ways to meet those goals, which is why we devote a chapter to it, and mention it in a couple of others.

The most common use that we think of is to replace the future income that a breadwinner of the family would have earned if he or she dies prematurely. That is an extremely important need, but it is not the only one, however; let's look at some others in this chapter.

Although we use the term "spouse" several times in this chapter, the concept also works for non-married partners.

With regards to life insurance being boring, apparently it is, based on one conversation I had in a social setting. I was telling an acquaintance that many people tell me my occupation, financial planning, is dull. She replied, "Oh that's not so bad. It's not like you're in life insurance!" There you have it.

Keep in mind, it does not have to be exciting to be important and beneficial.

Q **I don't need life insurance for my non-working spouse, do I?**

A **You may.** Even though the spouse does not earn a salary, there is a cost to replace services such as nanny, cleaning, handyman, and others. If you do not need those services, then you may not need the insurance. What if he or she were planning to go back to work at some point in the future? Factor in the loss of any future income he or she would have earned. The amount of death benefit needed will frequently be less than one for a breadwinner.

Q **I'm going to become part of a blended family.** How does life insurance fit in?

A **Let's say that you both have children from prior marriages.** What would happen if one of you dies? If the assets go only to the surviving spouse, the children of the deceased may be very unhappy. If the assets go only to the children, then the survivor may be very unhappy and possibly in a tough financial situation if they relied on the deceased spouse's income and investments while they were alive. Either way, problems occur. Here is where the insurance comes in. When you get married, you each buy a life insurance policy with your children or grandchildren as the beneficiaries. The other assets can then go to the surviving spouse and everyone is taken care of. Each family has its own dynamics and this concept can be structured differently, as needed. The key is to make sure everyone is taken care of. Do not rely on your current/ future spouse to provide for your children who are from a prior marriage, and vice versa. That is a huge mistake! Have your wishes set in stone via trusts/wills, beneficiary designations, and proper titling of assets.

In addition to what is described above, it may be necessary or advisable, to have insurance on each other for the benefit of the survivor. If there are not enough assets to provide for both of you throughout retirement, then this makes a lot of sense.

Q **Taxes are going up.** How can our life insurance help us with that?

A **Congress has allowed life insurance to maintain tremendous tax advantages.** One benefits the person while they are alive; the other upon death. The first is cash value. Permanent life insurance policies can be structured to accumulate cash value. That money grows tax-deferred. The owner of the policy may remove premiums and take loans from the policy without paying them back. The money is not taxable as long as the policy remains in force until death. The death benefit will decrease, but there is no taxable event.

The other tax benefit is the death benefit. When someone passes away the proceeds from life insurance are paid out income tax-free and, if properly structured, estate tax-free as well (for those who may have an estate tax problem). The cost of life insurance is usually pennies on the dollar (of coverage) per year. You're using leverage to buy it. Remember to work with a financial planner to determine whether these ideas work in your situation. They are not appropriate for everyone.

Q **I'm nervous we could lose everything if we get sued.** How can we protect some of our money?

A **Cash value accumulated within a permanent life insurance policy in some states is creditor protected.** Some states set limits on the dollar amount, and others do not. Each state is different, but for those where it is protected this can be a sound strategy for preventing creditors from getting a hold of the money. It may be the same with annuities in your state. Contact a financial advisor or attorney to verify your state's regulations. The policy needs to be kept for life. If it is not, an unfavorable tax consequence will likely occur.

Q **My spouse's assets are tied up in their business.** What if he/she passes away? I can't run their business!

A **There are a few scenarios that can be planned for in case a spouse who is a business owner passes away while still owning the business.** If there are partners, create a buy-sell agreement where each owner has a life insurance policy, which will provide the money to buy out the deceased owner's portion of the business. The agreement should state the policy must be used to fund the buy-out. This way the spouse can walk away with cash and not stress over having to deal with the business. Without the agreement, the spouse becomes involved in a business they're not familiar with. The co-owners probably would not like that!

If there are no other owners, then buy a life insurance policy on the owner with the spouse as beneficiary, so the spouse is taken care of and can have the money to either hire someone to run the business (long term or until a sale occurs), or close it down altogether.

If there are no other owners and the owner is not insurable, then the owner must save outside of the business, or through a work-related retirement plan. It takes years to accumulate enough, so begin as soon as possible—I cannot emphasize this enough.

Q **What if the spouse who owns/works in the business becomes disabled but does not die?**

A **The answer is long-term disability insurance.** The chances of becoming disabled are much higher than dying, during working years, and can be financially devastating if you are not prepared.

Q **I've heard the estate tax can take a large part of our money when we die.** Is that true and what can we do about it?

A **The estate tax can take a large bite out of a deceased person's wealth.**

The good news is that very few individuals, or couples are currently vulnerable to estate taxes, because there is an exemption of 11.58 million dollars per spouse (2020). Keep in mind that the law can change. Congress could reduce the exemption amount from current levels. As of 2020, if a single person, or the second of a couple, passes away any assets over the 11.58 million exemption amount are subject to a 40% tax. The second spouse may be able to use any unused exemption left over from the first spouse in addition to their own when they pass. The use of the first deceased spouse exemption doesn't

happen automatically, so seek professional guidance.
The exemption amount increases annually with inflation.

In an effort to minimize the effects of the estate tax, life insurance is frequently used in conjunction with an irrevocable trust to keep the death benefit outside the estate. The death benefit is not only exempt from estate taxes using this strategy, but is used to make up for the estate taxes paid for the rest of the estate, at a relatively low cost, compared to other methods of paying those taxes.

Chapter 11

Legacy Planning

Q **What is legacy planning?**

A **Legacy planning is a means of leaving your mark on the world, putting a plan in place to take care of generations behind you.** Many of us worry about what happens when we're not there. The plan we put in place takes care of our family and community that continues when we are gone. It's a way to make an impact when we're no longer here. It could involve helping your children. Perhaps you want to provide something for your grandchildren. Maybe there is a charity you benefited from or strongly believe in and want to support after you've gone.

I don't have children, and want whatever is left when I die to go to charities, and maintain my income while I'm still here. What can I do?

You can donate assets to charity and receive income for the rest of your life.

The use of a Charitable Remainder Trust provides income to the donor, who will also receive a tax deduction when the gift is made. You do not need to be a multi-millionaire to do this. Once the gift is made to the Charitable Remainder Trust, it's irrevocable. The underlying charity or charities that will ultimately receive the money can be changed, however.

The benefits, while you are alive, include up-front tax deduction if you itemize, removal of the donated assets from your estate (without paying capital gains on the asset), and potentially a larger stream of income (if the asset was not sold and taxed before the donation). Depending on how it is invested, the income received by the donor can be tax efficient, even income tax-free. (Keep in mind that at least 10% of the original principal must be left to go to the charity.)

A hypothetical example below compares the income generated for the donor through an outright sale of a stock, with zero cost basis, and a sale of the same stock within a Charitable Remainder Trust. Assumptions include 5% income and annual income for the life of the donor.

Outside Sale:	Charitable Remainder Trust Sale:
Sale price: $200,000	$200,000
Tax deduction for charitable contribution	
$0	$74,000
Subtract capital gains tax (top tax bracket)	
-$40,000	$0
Income:	
$160,000 x 5% = $8,000	$200,000 x 5% = $10,000

There are limits to the amount of charitable deduction a person can take in any one year. Speak with your tax preparer prior to donating.

 When we die, we want whatever is left to go to our children and charities. How do we accomplish this?

A great way to pass assets to both your children and charities would be to add a Wealth Replacement Trust along with the Charitable Remainder Trust (described in the prior question).

The income the donor receives can be used for two purposes. The money can be used for living expenses while the rest funds a life insurance policy held in the Wealth Replacement Trust.

When the donors pass away, the charity receives the assets in the Charitable Remainder Trust, and the children receive the life insurance proceeds income tax free. You've accomplished both goals while minimizing taxes and potential creditor threats to the money.

Q **We love our children and grandchildren, but don't want to spoil them with a large inheritance.** What do we do?

A **There are a couple of ways to reduce the risk of spoiling your children and grandchildren with an inheritance.** One is to spread out when they receive their inheritance, as opposed to giving them a lump-sum amount. Some investment or annuity companies allow the account owner to designate that beneficiaries must receive money over time. The beneficiary cannot change that stipulation when the owner passes away. A trust can also be used to designate certain ages when a beneficiary or beneficiaries receives the money. We will go into more detail on this later in the book in the chapter titled "Keeping Assets In Your Family If Your Child Is Financially Irresponsible."

The other method is to teach your heirs to be responsible with money. A good way to do that is to establish an endowment fund. (Again, you do not need to be wealthy to do this.) By establishing a Donor Advised Endowment Fund, money is given to the fund; that money is invested and either a percentage or dollar amount is paid out annually to the recipient. The donor can structure the fund to have their children and/or grandchildren determine which charities are the recipients of the annual donation. This way you teach philanthropy to your children. Imagine your children and grandchildren getting together once a year to discuss what organizations are going to receive your hard-earned money. If you think your children have been over-indulged and have no clue what the real world is like, this can become a great teaching tool.

A colleague of mine established a family rule to teach her daughter the importance of charitable giving. Every year, around the Holidays, she had her daughter give away some old toys and clothes to a shelter for abused children. The daughter got to choose what to give away. At first, the little girl didn't want to give anything away. It was hers! But, when she went to the shelter to give the gifts, she saw the excitement on the faces of the other children, who had very little of their own, and it changed her outlook. From then on she looked forward to her annual gifting. That's a great way to build character in young people.

 We want our money to go to our children when we die, but what are the best ways to accomplish that?

 There are a few things to consider when leaving money to heirs, including taxes and asset protection. Let's look at both of these.

IRAs and other qualified plans such as 401(k)s, 403(b)s, and 457(b)s are generally not good assets to pass to heirs. 100% of the money will be taxable at some point. Most beneficiaries of these plans choose to withdraw the money when they receive it, which means they take a tax hit right way. Few beneficiaries elect to make smaller annual withdrawals over a lifetime, which can add up to significantly more money received by the beneficiary. (The taxes paid are based upon ordinary income tax rates.)

Most 401(k)'s, some 403(b)'s, and any other retirement plans covered by ERISA (Employee Retirement Income Security Act of 1974) have full creditor protection, based on federal law. Defined benefit pension plans are included in this. IRAs have creditor protection up to a limit of $1,362,800 (in 2020) in case of bankruptcy. That amount will increase in 2022. State laws determine whether an IRA or Roth IRA is protected from non-bankruptcy creditors. Many states do not provide creditor protection for beneficiary IRAs, even if they do provide protection for the original owner of the IRA. Check your state law, as each state is different.

Better assets to transfer are after-tax accounts (also called non-qualified), which may be taxed at capital gains rates or ordinary income tax rates, depending on the investment. Capital gains tax rates are lower than ordinary income tax rates. In addition, they receive what is called a step-up in basis, which means that only the amount received that exceeds the dollar value of the investment on the date of death is subject to income taxes. Most lack creditor protection. Annuities and life insurance may be an exception to the lack of creditor protection. Check the rules in your state.

Roth IRAs allow for income tax-free distributions, but are similar to IRAs in their creditor protection, in many states, but not all.

Trusts can be helpful for passing money to heirs, as well. Wealth Replacement Trusts, also called Irrevocable Life Insurance Trusts are commonly used to leave money to heirs. The owner of the trust (grantor) gifts money to the trust. The beneficiaries of the trust use that money to buy a life insurance policy owned by the trust. When the grantor dies, the beneficiaries receive the death benefit from the life insurance policy, free of income and estate taxes. Irrevocable trusts provide asset protection for the creator of the trust because it is irrevocable, so the owner has no or limited access to the assets. Revocable trusts, which are the more common form of trust used today, do not have creditor protection for the grantor. There are other trusts which can be very useful for passing assets to heirs, but that is beyond the scope of this book.

Q **How do I make sure that the inheritance I leave my family stays in my family?**

A **If you want your children's inheritance to remain in your blood line, certain trusts can accomplish that.** If you do not plan properly, here's what can happen. Let's say for example, that your son Peter inherits your assets when you pass. If Peter passes away and his spouse Lisa remarries, the inheritance may go to her and then upon her death or divorce, to a future spouse of hers. If Peter and Lisa had children of their own, those children may be left out. A properly executed trust could allow for Lisa to use money while she is alive, but the remainder can come back to the family when she passes.

Q **How do we protect the money for our special needs child when we're gone?**

A **If you have a special needs child, who cannot make their own financial decisions, you will usually want to set up a trust that allows withdrawals for the needs of that person.** The trust holds title to the assets, which means it owns the assets, as opposed to an individual owning them. The money is used for the benefit of the child's health, education, maintenance and support. Creditors cannot access that money. The trustee (the person who administers the trust) is chosen by you and will oversee the trust and make distributions as necessary. The trustee can be a family member or an independent third party corporate trustee. There are benefits and drawbacks to both.

The benefit to having a family member be the trustee is that they will cost less than hiring an outside party to handle the responsibilities. They have the right to be paid for their service, but are typically less expensive than a corporate trustee. Family members acting as the trustee usually know the beneficiaries of the trust and may have an emotional bond that an outsider may not, potentially resulting in more attention and better care.

The disadvantage is that the family member may not have the skill set or desire to handle the requirements of a trustee. The family member may not be able to handle the requirements in the future—an example would be a parent who later in life develops health issues of their own. In some cases, family members may not have the child's best interest at heart. It is not unheard of for theft to occur from the trust. A corporate trustee typically has the experience and professionalism to handle the required tasks.

Q **We have children from prior marriages.** How does that impact our legacy planning?

A **Plan early.** If there are children from prior marriages in your family, it is vital to have a conversation about what the two of you want to happen with your money when you pass away. Who would you like to receive your assets if you pass away first or second? This should be discussed, agreed upon, and put in writing. There are numerous sad stories of spouses or children who received nothing, or very little, when their loved-ones passed away, because of improper planning. It may be because of a mistake, or could be intentional.

Let's take an example of John and Jane. They are married and in their late 70s. Both were married once before, and they have two children, each from prior marriages. John passes away and it turns out he never changed his beneficiaries on an old life insurance policy and an IRA. Jane contacts the life insurance company and finds out that John's ex-wife is the beneficiary.

She next contacts his IRA provider and discovers that John's children are the beneficiaries. Jane knew the house would go to the children once she passed, but nothing was put in place to ensure that she had the right to stay there. His children would decide whether they let her stay in the house. Jane needs those three assets to maintain her standard of living. John had told her those were to go to her. Most states do have some sort of spousal elective share claim, so she may be able to inherit some assets that way. Beyond that, all Jane can do is to try to take this to court.

There are two viewpoints when we look at blended families and inheritances. The first is the spouse and the second are the children from the other spouse's prior marriages. John's children may look at this situation and say that they are John's children and deserve the IRA while Jane was only married to him for a few years. Perhaps they think she married him for financial security reasons. Maybe they are right. Jane sees it differently. She took care of John for the last 3 years while his health declined. Where were his children? They didn't help at all. They rarely called and almost never visited him. These are real world issues that frequently occur. Many people feel this sort of thing will never happen in their family. A saying in estate planning is that you never truly know someone until you've shared an estate with them. A little communication and some follow-up can help mitigate these problems.

John and Jane should have both updated beneficiaries on their individually-owned investment accounts (such as IRAs, 401(k) s and pensions), as well as life insurance, and shown each other the confirmation statements from the beneficiary updates. A trust could designate what other property goes to the spouse and what goes to the children. It's best to tell all parties what will happen, so there is minimal tension in the family upon death. John could have designated some property to go to his kids. Assuming both spouses are in reasonable health, they could buy life insurance policies to make sure the children are taken care of, and the surviving spouse can receive the other assets.

John may not have wanted Jane to inherit one or more of the accounts from him. If that is the case, again, communicate with all affected parties.

Q **My spouse has significantly more money than I do.** How do I protect myself from all the assets going to his children from a prior marriage if he dies first?

A **Just as with the question above, have the conversation about what happens when each of you passes.** Ask your spouse what his or her intentions are if he or she passes first. If your spouse says it goes somewhere else or to someone besides you, but you need the money, then discuss it. A life insurance policy on the spouse's life may be very helpful here. Make sure you own it, so that only you can cancel it, or if a trust owns it, be sure to be listed as a party to be notified if any changes are made to it. If your spouse says it goes to you when he or she passes, make sure you see that in writing. Trust but verify!

Q **I'm getting remarried.** How can I protect the inheritance for my children from a prior marriage if I die first?

A **First determine how much of your assets you want to go to your children when you die.** Make your children the beneficiaries on those accounts or policies if possible. Keep in mind that 401(k)s and some other retirement plans are subject to governmental requirements and your spouse has to sign a form waiving his or her right to those accounts. IRAs do not have that requirement; and are therefore the easiest way. For other assets, having a trust where you are the sole owner with the children as beneficiaries will work. Assets owned within the trust will go to those beneficiaries. Irrevocable trusts work better in this situation.

A change of residency from one state to another can give the spouse greater inheritance rights than they previously had. Each state has different spousal election inheritance rights, so if you move out of state, it may impact your children's inheritance if you predecease your spouse, as the surviving spouse may have a right to a higher percentage of the assets than were initially planned on.

We are in a committed relationship, but not married. How does that affect our planning?

Nothing will automatically go to your significant other upon your passing, and vice versa, unless you reside in a state that follows Common Law. If that is the case, you will need to be able to prove the Common Law Marriage existed. If you can prove it, you may be eligible for social security, pension, and life insurance benefits. These situations make proper planning all the more important. Verify you both have designated each other as beneficiaries on the assets you want to pass to each other. Name them in your trust or will. Same with anyone else to whom you want to leave something.

There may be tax consequences for larger estates as there are no exemptions to estate taxes for non-married couples. For those few who are subject to estate taxes, the rate is 40%, so proper planning must be done. Estates under $11.58 million (2020) for an individual are exempt from this tax.

Chapter 12

Keeping Assets In Your Family If Your Child Is Financially Irresponsible

Q **I want to leave money to my adult child, but they will just spend it as soon as they receive it.** What can I do?

A **So, you don't want your adult children to spend all your hard-earned money on, say a sports car or other toys?** Maybe you don't agree with their lifestyle choices. Or, possibly you do not want to support their addiction, be it gambling or drugs. Perhaps they have a mental illness that may affect their ability to wisely handle their own finances. Regardless of the reason, some people are just financially irresponsible and cannot be trusted with large sums of money.

One way to control that spending is with a spendthrift trust. Let us look at an example. Your 25-year old son Johnny has a gambling addiction. He's spent all his money and has asked you repeatedly to help him out. You love him in spite of the frustration of watching him struggle. If you leave him money to which he has unrestricted access, then you know it will all be gone by the end of football season. A spendthrift trust designates a person or company (the trustee), to determine how much and for what purpose Johnny can receive money from the trust. Health, welfare, education, and maintenance are valid uses. These include mortgage or rent, college tuition, utilities, etc. The trustee will not give unlimited sums to pay gambling debts or other wasteful expenses. There is a cost to establishing the trust and maintaining it, including the trustee compensation, especially if it is a company.

Age bands can be used by a trust to provide money to Johnny at certain ages. Could be 1/3 at age 25, 1/3 at age 35, and 1/3 at age 45, or whatever is most suitable for the situation. The idea is that as he ages, he may be more mature and responsible.

If it's a maturity issue, and not an addiction or mental incapacity, then you may be able to teach your children to become financially responsible. One interesting way to do so is to create an endowment and Charitable Remainder Trust. Refer to the chapter on Legacy Planning for a description of that.

Q **How can you avoid paying for your child's rehab?**

A **The key is to identify the potential for a problem before the addiction occurs.** This is easier said than done, but is no different than other types of planning and just as important! One of the most common reasons for a child's substance abuse (or other addictions) is agony after their parent's divorce. The other most common reason is over-medication after an accident/surgery or traumatic event. I will focus on the divorce aspect for this answer, but the way to address the others is similar.

When going into a relationship with a partner who has children, ask yourself the following questions. Is either parent blowing their children off after the divorce? Perhaps the parent is spending that time with you, or the other parent with their significant other. Are you or your ex ignoring your children? This may all seem insignificant, but kids can be deeply affected, with dire consequences.

A scenario can look like the following: After the divorce of her parents, Jill felt ignored and unlovable. Not knowing how to cope, she started experimenting with drugs. Meanwhile, Jill's father got remarried to a nice woman named Jane. Jill continued her drug usage and eventually got hooked on heroin. Ultimately Jill's addiction resulted in her father and Jane getting robbed and ending up divorced due to the constant stress. Sounds crazy, but it happens, and occurs at all income levels. Children's mental health issues should be monitored. It's also worth looking into how mental health is being managed.

If you're considering dating someone who's divorced, one thing you can do is note if his or her children are getting the proper attention post-divorce. If not, some children could act out in order to get a parent back into their life. Pay attention to who the child hangs out with for clues of trouble.

Encourage therapy as a lower cost way of avoiding rehab. A little time, care and money can save tens of thousands of dollars and a lot of stress down the road, if behavioral issues are not addressed.

Chapter 13

Protect Your Children's College Money

Q How should we save for our children's college expenses?

A 529 Plans, Coverdell Education Savings Accounts, and Uniform Transfers To Minors Act (UTMA)/ Uniform Gift To Minors Act (UGMA) custodial accounts are the more common savings vehicles for your children or grand children's college expenses.

What do you mean by, "Protect your children's college money." Whom should I be protecting them from?

There can be a need to protect your children's college money from your spouse, future spouse, significant other, spouse's significant other, general creditors, etc. The concerns center around theft, bankruptcy, and lawsuits. One might think college savings would be protected, but that is not necessarily the case.

What protections are there in those savings plans?

Coverdell Education Savings Accounts are exempt from bankruptcy laws if the contributions were made at least one year prior to the bankruptcy. 529 College Savings Plans work differently. They are based on state law. About half of the states offer protection and half do not. Of the ones that do, most only provide protection for 529 Plans based in that state. Only a few provide protection for 529 Plans from other states. Some provide protection for the donor, some the beneficiary, and some the owner. In order to find out what protections are in place in your state, contact an attorney in that state who practices in bankruptcy law. The UTMA, or Uniform Transfers to Minors Act, or UGMA, Uniform Gifts to Minors Act protects the money from the parent's creditors because the money is not accessible by the parent. The child, 18 or older, may have their own creditors and the account may be subject to garnishment when they are legally an adult.

Q **What else can I do to protect their college money?**

A **One major concern for the protection of your children's college money is theft.** It could be from your spouse, significant other, the children themselves, or a friend. Unfortunately, it can and has happened. An example we have seen is that someone's ex-spouse had a new significant other, who obtained the social security numbers of the children and depleted their college savings accounts before leaving the relationship. In order to help prevent this, do not discuss accounts with a new partner. It's important to hide and not share your passwords and statements with a significant other too early. Over time, you may decide to relax your caution, but early on, there is no reason these vital pieces of information should be available or shared. You may be able to add additional security measures, if the company which custodies the money will allow.

Chapter 14

Long Term Care Protection

Q **What does this have to do with protecting myself, my children, and my assets, as well as dating?**

A **If you are in a relationship later in life, married or not, the problems associated with long term care will likely be present at some point.** This is one of the biggest risks to a retiree's money while they are alive. Long-term care services can be quite expensive. According to the Genworth Cost of Care Survey 2019, on a national level, the median cost for assisted living is $48,612 per year. A semi-private nursing home room costs $90,155, and a private nursing home room costs $102,200 per year.

75% of single and 50% of married couples will deplete all their savings after paying for just one year of care. Assets spent paying for long-term care may leave a surviving partner with little money to support themselves. Most likely adult children are not in a position to be able to provide the care themselves.

Q **What is Long Term Care?**

A **Long term care is the service and support you may need to meet your health or personal care needs over a long period of time, if you are not able to do them for yourself, according to the U.S. Department of Health and Human Services.** Most of the care is assistance with personal tasks of everyday life. These include Activities of Daily Living, such as bathing, dressing, using the toilet, transferring to or from a bed or chair, caring for incontinence, and eating. Some people may need help due to cognitive disorders, such as dementia or Alzheimer's disease. Other causes are accidents, illness, advanced age, strokes, and other chronic conditions. We think of elderly people when we think of those with long-term care needs. More often than not, that is the case. However, 37% of those receiving long-term care services are under age 65.

Q **At what age should I look into this?**

A **Once you are in your 50s, it is important to look at how to protect against the high costs of long-term care.** (There is nothing wrong with addressing it in your forties, either.) The longer you wait, the more expensive it becomes to protect against the high costs of long-term care. Those in their 60s and up will see the cost of protection rise rapidly.

Q **My parents didn't need assistance with long term care, so why should I be concerned?**

A **Not everyone will need long-term care.**
Some people pass away without a period of decline, such as from a heart attack, stroke, accident, etc. The statistics indicate that 2/3 of 65-year-olds will need long-term care at some point in their remaining life. The fact that your parents did not require care does not eliminate the chance that you will need it. People are living longer. Health problems that were once fatal, may not be anymore. The longer we live, the more prone we are to needing assistance. Do not expect to have the same situation as your parents.

Q **Won't Medicare and/or Medicaid pay for long-term care costs that I may incur?**

A **Medicare may provide a limited amount for long-term care costs.** Medicaid may require a spend-down of assets before they will pay anything. Here is how they work. In order to qualify for Medicare to pay for long-term care expenses, one must have a recoverable situation, have been in the hospital for three days or longer, be at least 65 years old, and be in a skilled nursing facility. If you meet those qualifications, then Medicare will pay 100% of the first 20 days stay, 80% for the next 80 days, and nothing thereafter. Considering the average time someone needs long-term care services is between two and three years, 100 days just does not provide much. Many people would not qualify because their situation is not recoverable or they did not have a three-day hospital stay.

Medicaid is for the indigent. You will have to spend your assets down to a small amount in order to qualify to receive Medicaid benefits. Each state has its own rules on Medicaid long-term care eligibility and coverage. One major reason for not wanting to rely on Medicaid to pay for long-term care costs is that you have less choice on where your long-term care needs will be met. Not all facilities are created equal.

Years ago I worked in a consulting capacity and was reviewing files of nursing home operators. Some of the files contained health reports from the state that listed problems various patients had incurred in the facilities. Examples include "patient found lying in their own urine," or "rashes found all over a patient." These were due to lack of proper care/supervision at the facilities. Ideally, you want to have control over which facility you go to. When you rely on Medicaid, you may lose that control.

A colleague of mine found a facility for her mother that she really liked. The place said they had a 2-year waiting list. My colleague told them she was paying privately, not via the government. The next day she received a call that they had an opening. Private pay gives more choice.

Q **Are my assets at risk if my spouse needs long term care, even if we keep our assets separate and have a prenuptial agreement?**

A **Your assets may be at risk.** Even if you keep assets separate and have a prenuptial agreement, you may be responsible for paying for your spouse's care. Here's why. A spouse (or other family members if there is no spouse) may be responsible for long term care expenses based on Filial Responsibility Laws or Filial Support Laws. Though they are rarely enforced, 29 states and Puerto Rico have these laws on the books. The law typically states that a spouse, parent, or child of an impoverished person has a responsibility to care for or financially assist that person. The reason they are rarely enforced is because once Medicare, Social Security, and Medicaid were enacted to offer a safety net to seniors, Filial Laws became less important.

As of the time of the writing of this book, efforts to significantly reduce funding for Medicaid by some politicians are in the works. If that happens, these laws may be enforced much more frequently.

The 29 states and 1 territory that have Filial Responsibility or Support Laws include Alaska, Kentucky, New Jersey, Tennessee, Arkansas, Louisiana, North Carolina, Utah, California, Maryland, North Dakota, Vermont, Connecticut, Massachusetts, Ohio, Virginia, Delaware, Mississippi, Oregon,

West Virginia, Georgia, Montana, Pennsylvania, Indiana, Nevada, Rhode Island, Puerto Rico, Iowa, New Hampshire and South Dakota.

Q **My children and spouse/partner are my long-term care plan.** What more do I need?

A **Back in the day when people had large families that stayed close to each other, this was how long-term care was handled.** People also did not live as long as they do today.

The world has changed. Families are smaller, spread out geographically, and typically both spouses work. Often people have children later in life that may still be at home when a parent needs care. All of those reasons make it far less likely that your children can care for you. Spouses are often too feeble themselves to be able to assist. Can you lift your husband if he falls? Can you help your spouse out of the bathtub? If you're in your eighties or older, can you lift your wife? It is not realistic to think your family will be able to care for you. Even if they can, it often causes depression among family caregivers. Two friends of mine cared for their fathers for a period of time. Both ended up on depression medication. One of them started seeing a therapist. Do you want that to happen to your children? You are much better off having a plan in place to pay for long-term care.

My friends don't have anything in place for this.
Why should I?

Do not assume that your friends are in the same situation as you, even if there are some similarities.
Their financial and family dynamics may be different than yours. They may not be financially astute. Perhaps they have not disclosed the entire story to you. Make a decision on what to do about how to pay for long-term care based on your situation, not someone else's. An intelligent decision can be made only if you have all the facts. You do not have that with your friends. Think of it like this, if all your friends smoke, should you? Is it less risky because friends smoke? Of course not. Make decisions based on what's best for your interests.

I have more than enough money to pay for any care I might need. Is there any reason to protect against long-term care costs?

There is. Wealthy people can afford to self-insure, but that does not mean it is a good idea. Weigh the cost versus the benefit of long-term care protection and it will typically cost much less to pass the financial risk on to another party. There is always the chance you may never need it.

Q How do you protect against the high costs of long-term care?

A **The best way to protect yourself against long-term care costs is to pass those costs on to an insurance company.** That way the catastrophic risk of paying for multiple years of care is removed or decreased. There are a few ways to do this. They include long-term care insurance, life insurance with a long-term care rider, and an annuity with a long-term care rider. An individual or couple could opt for one of these for each or they could be blended together.

Remember that on average assisted living could cost you $43,539 per year. A point to keep in mind is that the benefits you'd receive will likely exceed all the premiums you pay.

An individual can pay premiums for a long term care policy for 20 years, and if they go on claim with the insurance company from that point forward, the benefits received from the company will likely exceed all premiums paid (for that 20-year period) in less than one year.

Q I heard that I should get long term care insurance, is that true?

A **You should have a plan for how to pay for long-term care.** A realistic plan! Long-term care insurance is one way to pay for long-term care costs. It is a good method to pay for care, but not the only one. The other two, as mentioned previously, are life insurance with a long-term care rider, or an annuity with a long-term care rider. There are benefits and drawbacks with each. If someone does not have the money to pay premiums, they are not a candidate for any of these three. Long term care insurance is the most efficient method of paying for care while protecting yourself, but if you do not use it, you typically lose it, meaning the money you spent on premiums will not go back to your heirs. With the other two methods, someone will benefit from them if the original owner does not need it for long-term care. There are other differences as well, so speak with a financial advisor who is knowledgeable about all three.

I was on a flight once and struck up a conversation with the gentleman sitting next to me. I knew something was up when he smiled when I told him I'm a financial planner. The usual reaction is one of boredom or apathy. He was a long-term care insurance salesperson. One of my first questions was whether he provided all three types of coverage or only long-term care insurance. He glossed over the other two methods. The problem with this reaction is that not everyone is a fit for long-term care insurance. One of the other two may be better. There is usually more than one way to accomplish a financial goal. Find an advisor who will meet your needs. Not one who will try to fit you into their business.

Q Is there an age that is too old to protect against long-term care costs?

A **There is.** Eighty to 85 years of age is typically the maximum to pass the risks/costs onto an insurance company. This may change at any time, so check with a financial advisor or agent who works with these policies.

Q How long should I expect to need long-term care?

A **The average length of time that care is required is between two and three years, with some lasting ten or more.** Alzheimer's, dementia, strokes, Parkinson's, spinal injuries, and others can lead to long periods of required care.

Q What if my spouse or I don't qualify for any of these forms of long-term care protection?

A **Poor health or exceeding the maximum age limit, may eliminate those as options for you.** One thing you can do is purchase an annuity that has an enhanced rider benefit, which does not require a health exam for qualification. The benefit increases the amount you may receive if you have qualifying long-term care needs. Each insurance company has their own requirements for determining the need. The benefit is not nearly as strong as the other choices listed previously, but it may be better than nothing.

Chapter 15

Mistakes Investors Make

Q **My spouse handles the investing and finances.**
I hate that stuff. Do I need to be involved?

A **Unfortunately you do, at least to some degree.**
If you do not have a clue what is happening as your
spouse handles the finances, you are a much easier victim if your
spouse should plan a divorce and wants to take advantage. You
do not need to make the decisions, but you should keep copies
of your assets (yours and your spouse's), and anything you sign.
Keep full copies, not just the first or last page. That includes
your tax returns. The more involved you become, the easier it
will be to identify if your spouse is a crook, incompetent, is not
doing anything, is overly risky, or perhaps too conservative with
the money.

Let's look at an example of Robert and Katy. Katy is very good
with the finances and investments. Robert does not have a clue

what they own. He signs whatever Katy tells him to and pays little attention to what he's actually signing. Little does he know that Katy is having an extramarital relationship. She decides to leave Robert and hides some of the assets prior to leaving him. She plans it for quite some time. How will Robert know what was hidden? She may have liquidated bank accounts and left Robert with no money to pay his bills. His life will be in shambles for quite some time until he gets back on his feet. He has no money to pay lawyer fees for the divorce while Katy hires an expensive attorney. This may sound far-fetched, but it isn't. Law enforcement officials see this happen. Had Robert kept copies of all accounts and tax returns, he would be in a better position to notice if something was going wrong.

Q **My spouse never wants to discuss finances.** He/she gets so angry, I just stopped asking. What do I do?

A **I see this happen with couples, sometimes.** The question is, why is it they're getting upset? Is it because of financial difficulties? Or, maybe the spouse doesn't want to reveal what they have? Perhaps something illegal is going on. Each of these requires a different approach. Ideally you both have discussed finances prior to marriage, so you have had these discussions before, which should make it easier to discuss during marriage. Assuming that is not the case here, or your spouse no longer will have a civil discussion, and will not reveal investments that they or you both have, then try the following.

Look at any hard copies of your bank/investment statements, if your spouse keeps hard copies of them. If you have joint accounts, go to the bank or investment company and ask to see a copy of your accounts. I've repeated this a few times in this book, but again, look at your tax return, it will tell you volumes. Check with your mortgage company and confirm you're not late on payments. You do not want any surprise foreclosure notices! If you believe your spouse is hiding anything or perhaps doing something illegal, it may be worth hiring a private investigator to do some research for you. It will cost some money but may save you quite a bit more, in the long run, if your gut instinct is correct. Many times it is.

Start saving on your own, if you have not been doing so meet with a financial planner. At least you will have something and some control.

Q **I have a 401(k) and insurance…that's good enough, isn't it?**

A **It is a start to getting your finances in order, but it is not enough.** There is much more to a well-rounded financial plan than simply having a 401(k) retirement savings plan at work and health insurance. Financial planning is made up of an overall plan and its various components. These include insurance, investments, taxes, retirement planning, and estate planning. Everyone's situation is different, so speak with a financial planner about your individual needs. I will address each of the components individually.

Financial Plan

If you don't have a plan, how do you know if you are on target to meeting your goals for the lifestyle you want to have throughout the rest of your life? What are your goals? A 401(k) and some insurance doesn't tell you if it's likely you'll run out of money 10 years before you pass away. It doesn't tell you whether you will pay unnecessary taxes. How will you afford to pay for care if you develop a long-term health condition, such as Alzheimer's?

Insurance

Insurance is not just health insurance. Health insurance is important, but let's not forget life, disability, umbrella liability, long-term care, auto, homeowners, renters, and commercial insurances for businesses. There are others as well, but this list is a good start. Do you have enough coverage, or too much coverage?

Investments

Investments have many purposes. They may be used to generate income for you to live on, or to grow your nest egg, or both. They can be used for preservation of your money, even speculation. All kinds of investments are available to meet your needs.

Do your existing investments align with your goals and overall financial plan? Do you have enough liquid savings to cover emergencies and/or a job loss?

Retirement planning

Retirement planning includes your 401(k), but there's more to consider. Is it better to contribute to a Roth IRA or 401(k) than a traditional 401(k)? Perhaps both should be used. Does your employer provide matching dollars on your 401(k)? If so, are you contributing at least enough to receive the full match from the employer? Are you self-employed? If you are, there are some retirement savings vehicles that may be very beneficial. Do you have a good pension? If not, how will you replace your income when you retire? Social security is not enough. Are you on-target with your savings to maintain your standard of living? It is very important to know the answer to this.

Taxes

Tax planning has to do with reducing the amount of taxes paid over your lifetime. Are you taking advantage of all the deductions available to you? Is it better to pay taxes now or defer those taxes to sometime in the future? The answer to these questions can have a major impact on your retirement and financial success for the rest of your life. Make sure you consult with a tax professional.

Estate Planning

Do you have a trust or a will? If you're in an accident or have an illness, and end up on life support, should the doctor pull the plug or not? Who will process your trust/will when you pass away? Who gets your money and possessions when you pass away? Are you taking advantage of the most tax-efficient methods of passing money to the next generation? This is estate planning. Your finances have not been fully addressed if you have not taken these questions into consideration and prepared.

There are many more questions that can be asked regarding the topics listed. The point is, spend a little time developing a financial plan (with an expert in that field) and you will likely be much happier in the long run.

Q **We lost money due to poor investments.** I don't want to invest any longer, just save. Is that realistic?

A **If you have enough money saved, then you may be able to sit in cash or cash-equivalent investments.** Generally, cash-only options are not a good choice with all of your money. Each dollar will buy you half as much every 20 years, assuming just 3% inflation. For a 95-year-old, inflation is not going to be much of a concern. For a 60-year-old, relying on that money to pay the bills, inflation paints an ominous picture. Significantly less money may be left to heirs as well.

It's understandable that from an emotional standpoint, you have no desire to risk losing significant money again. As a financial planner, I would ask what happened to cause the loss. Perhaps it was timing, maybe you invested too aggressively. Regardless, do not allow a past bad experience to keep you from investing. If you get into a car accident, are you never going to drive again? If you lose your job, are you going to permanently stop working?

Of course not. Why should investing be any different? You learn from past mistakes. Make adjustments where necessary, but you don't necessarily need to make radical adjustments.

The adjustments could include changes to your risk level. For example, your could have some money in cash, some in moderate-risk investments, and perhaps some in aggressive investments. That way you are not putting it all at risk, but still have the potential to keep up with inflation. A portion of your money can be invested so that the principal is protected. The important point to take away from here is that there are a variety of ways to mitigate risk while investing, and still giving yourself an opportunity to earn more than a savings account would return.

 We're going to work on our financial plan next (summer, holiday, etc). What's wrong with waiting until then?

If that day is one or two weeks from now, fine. But if not, let's call it what it is-procrastination. There are a million excuses for not working on your finances, but every day you delay is a day you will never get back! Pick a day coming up shortly and make this your top priority for that day. Delaying your financial planning has a cost. Lost returns on money not invested, higher cost of insurance based on older age of application, etc. Schedule an appointment with a financial planner — that may give you the motivation to prepare for the appointment.

Q **I've read that certain investments are bad.**
Are they?

A **Over the years, I have read about, and heard many people say that certain categories of investments should be avoided.** Products are like tools in a tool belt. They are not good or bad. They were designed for a reason—to accomplish a goal. Some of them get a lot of use, others very little use. No one product will solve every problem you have. Building a financial strategy is like building a house. It takes a variety of tools. Just because a hammer is not necessary for one job, it doesn't mean you should always avoid using a hammer. The same goes for investments. Unfortunately, some advisors promote the use of certain investments that may not be the best tool to use or in amounts that exceed what is best for the client. There are bad apples in every industry.

Some investments are high-cost. Even so, they may be the least expensive method of accomplishing your goal, or the only method. If that is the case, use it; if not, go a less expensive route.

Many publications give advice that appears to make a lot of sense. Being in the industry, I have read and noticed that many magazine and newspaper articles are biased, whether for or against what they are writing about. Often, several points in these articles are very misleading or even completely wrong. The authors are usually unlicensed, not liable for what they write, and want to stir up emotions to get published and generate advertising dollars. I have even seen them write a negative article and at the bottom of the article acknowledge they benefit from an investment they own, if the subject they wrote against does poorly. Giving a balanced, educational article is not their goal. I advise you to always think critically and verify. You can't always take an article as 100% factual, but it should motivate you to ask more questions!

Q **I'm getting remarried.** We each have our own investments and will keep them separate. What issues should we be aware of?

A **There are several scenarios you both will want to discuss.** Do you each have enough money to cover your expenses and maintain your lifestyle? What if one of you does not, or years down the road, one of you runs out of money? When the first of you dies, who gets the deceased spouse's assets? When the survivor dies, who gets the assets? Will you have a prenuptial agreement?

Q **We are hiring a financial advisor.** What should we look out for?

A **How does the advisor conduct the appointment?** Does he or she get to know you before making suggestions about investments? Has he or she asked what your goals are? Is there a strategy involved? Does he or she give a few choices of what to do to meet your goals? Is the advisor product-focused?

Ideally you should be doing most of the talking. The advisor asks the questions, then sits back and listens, and asks follow-up questions. Once the advisor understands your goals, family, work, and financial situation, then they are in a position to put together strategies to meet those goals. That is what you should be looking for. Keep in mind, experience matters!
Rookie mistakes can have significant consequences for the rest of your life.

Make sure the advisor does what he or she claims. A lot of people hold themselves out as advisors, but many focus only on one product. You also will want to make sure the advisor is licensed.

It's kind of like if you're getting your kitchen renovated and call out for bids. Imagine if one of the contractors was to show up with only a hammer. That's his only tool. But, the other contractor comes with a full set of tools on his tool belt, and a bunch more in his truck. All else being equal, which one would you hire? Even if the person with the hammer is very talented with that tool, a renovation project requires a set of tools to get the job done right. An advisor that has a variety of tools can pick the ones that best accomplish your goals.

How can you tell if the advisor actually does what he/she says? Check what licenses and designations they have. Ask your advisor what percent of their business comes from investments, insurance, annuities, and so on. That will tell you a lot. Does he/she work with a team?

Do a background check on the Financial Industry Regulatory (FINRA) website, www.FINRA.org. Click on the box listed as "Broker Check." Most advisors will be listed on there or are registered with the SEC, www.adviserinfo.sec.gov.

If not licensed in securities or as a registered advisor, then the advisor may be very limited and not able to provide most investments.

Check if your advisor is insurance licensed. Some will be insurance licensed but not securities licensed. Many fall into this category. If they do, they may not be financial advisors—they cannot provide the solutions to many problems, and do not have more than one or two tools in their tool belt. You are better off seeking an advisor who meets the qualifications described above. What designations do they have? There are many, but the most noteworthy are: Certified Financial Planner™ (CFP®), Charter Financial Analyst (CFA), Chartered Financial Consultant (ChFC®), and Certified Investment Management Analyst˚ (CIMA®). For overall financial planning, look for the Certified Financial Planner™ (CFP®) designation. If you know nothing else about an advisor, except that he/she has one of these designations, at least you know he/she has had formal education, experience, and testing in the field.

Let's look at three of the more common ways an advisor gets paid. One of them is fee-based as a percentage of dollars under management or a flat fee. Another is a set fee based on hours spent, or by the project. The third is commission-based. Some advisors work strictly on one, others a combination. It does not matter which they use, as long as it is disclosed. Do not rely solely on cost or payment style in deciding who to use as an advisor. It is one of the factors, but not the only one. (Not even the most important). What does matter is the quality and value they bring to the table—are they fully licensed and certified, how much experience do they have, do they have a full set of tools at their disposal, do they listen to you and advise you based on your unique needs.

Q **My friend (neighbor, relative, etc.)** is very knowledgeable and helps me with my investments and finances. Why would I need a paid advisor?

A **There are several reasons to get professional help with your investments and/or financial planning.** The person assisting you (who is not in the business) may be knowledgeable and have the best intentions, but is not liable for their advice. That person is unlicensed, with no formal training in the industry. His or her area of knowledge may be limited to one area of interest, which could cause problems in your overall financial picture. For example, they may be great with certain investments, but cause problems with your taxes, estate plan, asset protection goals, etc. These are all related, but most people are not familiar with how each affects the other. Your friend may have a different risk tolerance and financial situation than you, which may result in recommendations inappropriate for your needs and goals.

Over the years, I've heard "hot tips" from clients that they were sure would pay off tremendously. I recall one client told me after the fact, that she had put $30,000 in a stock that "almost can't lose" based on a friend's recommendation. Well, it did lose. Luckily because of long-term planning we had done, the client could recover from losing that amount of money. What if that same friend had given other financial advice?

Think about it this way—if you had a serious health issue and a friend who wasn't a healthcare professional told you what to do, would you avoid going to the doctor and follow your friend's advice? Probably not. You may tell the doctor what your friend said and let the doctor respond, but ultimately it would be smart to follow the physician's recommendation. It's a good idea to get a second opinion and ask friends about their experiences, but in finance as in healthcare you should still seek a professional opinion.

Course

Would you be interested in an e-learning course that expands upon the concepts in this book?

Let us know by going to:
www.datingafterdivorcebook.com/course

If we receive enough interest, we will create an e-learning course.

Sources

www.al.com, Common Law Marriage, 12/28/2016, by Leaeda Gore.

www.bankrate.com/brm/news/sav/20000118.asp

www.bankrate.com/brm/prenup.asp

www.equalityinmarriage.org/bmbringup.html

www.family.findlaw.com/marriage/common-law-marriage.html

www.irahelp.com

Journal of Financial Planning,"Estate Planning Implications of Remarriage", February 2016, By John J. Scroggin.

www.keeblerandassociates.com/

www.longtermcare.gov/medicare-medicaid-more/medicaid/medicaid-eligibility/general-medicaid-requirements/

www.longtermcare.gov/medicare-medicaid-more/medicaid/medicaid-eligibility/financial-requirements/

www.longtermcare.gov/medicare-medicaid-more/medicaid/medicaid-eligibility/financial-requirements-assets/

www.longtermcare.gov/medicare-medicaid-more/medicaid/medicaid-eligibility/considerations-for-married-people/

www.longtermcare.gov/medicare-medicaid-more/medicaid/medicaid-eligibility/share-of-cost/

Prenups For Lovers, A Romantic Guide To Prenuptial Agreements

www.proassetprotection.com/

www.ssa.gov, Social Security Administration

Estate Planning For Unmarried Couples-A presentation by Michael J Tucker, Attorney, www.family.findlaw.com

Insure.com, http://www.insure.com/health-insurance/domestic-partner.html

Netquote.com. http://www.netquote.com/health-insurance/news/health-insurance-for-domestic-partners

National Conference of State Legislators, http://www.ncsl.org/research/human-services/civil-unions-and-domestic-partnership-statutes.aspx

Thebalance.com, www.thebalance.com/unlimied-marital-deduction-3505622

About The Authors

James M. Graham

James M. Graham has been a financial planner since 1996. He is a Certified Financial Planner™ and has been assisting people in managing their wealth, preserving it, and distributing it during their life and beyond in the most tax-advantageous way. Jim works with a team whose specialties include tax, legal, estate, insurance, investment, and financial planning. He uses these resources and his experience, to help his clients protect themselves, their children, and their assets. He believes in being a partner for the financial interests of his clients by developing long-term relationships that focus on strategy first. Jim was formerly the host of "Hey Jim!," a radio show dedicated to financial education.

www.orangerockwealthmanagement.com

Catherine Oneil

Catherine Oneil is an intuitive counselor, hypnotist, writer, teacher, lecturer and speaker who enjoys making people more conscious of their relationship choices. She has worked for the courts as a licensed counselor and has seen firsthand how people get in trouble when not seeing who they have attracted into their lives. She has also published courses that have been accepted in several states for training police officers. She is adjunct faculty member at the college level for counseling as well as for the police academy. In addition, she has written about relationships for several years for a national newspaper.

Catherine also has a great deal of experience working with addictions. She has worked at a state agency, DUI school, drug rehabs as well as large hospitals. Catherine has a passion for helping people be more aware in their relationships so that their children do not have to suffer the consequences. Catherine works with individuals, families, and couples.

Catherine2021@yahoo.com

Industry Disclosures

Investment advisory services offered through Clarus Wealth Advisors LLC, a SEC Registered Investment Advisor. Securities offered through Crown Capital Securities LP Member FINRA/SIPC. Clarus Wealth Advisors LLC and Crown Capital Securities LP are unaffiliated companies.

State and federal laws change frequently and the information in this book may not reflect the most recent changes. Please consult with an attorney, tax professional, and financial advisor for the most up-to-date advice.

This is not legal or tax advice and is not a substitute for legal or tax advice.

Made in the USA
Monee, IL
23 November 2020

48579479R00100